In the Same Way, Learn

Having a Teachable Spirit

Elaine Oostra

Bible Study for Young Adult Girls

Published by Field of View Press
Parma, Idaho

Cover designed by Elaine Oostra
Edited by JoEllen Claypool

For more information or additional copies, please contact:
Field of View Press
P.O. Box 1087
Parma, Idaho
fieldofviewpress@gmail.com

First printing 2017

Second printing 2018

ISBN: 13:978-0-9972316-2-5

Library of Congress Control Number – 2017909814

DEDICATION

Dedicated to my beautiful granddaughters, Kennady, Anna, Katie and Ellie my first great-granddaughter!
Psalm 25:5 "Lead me in your truth and teach me, for you are the God of my salvation; for you I will wait all day long."

Elaine Oostra

TABLE OF CONTENTS

IN THE SAME WAY, LEARN
Having a Teachable Spirit
(includes leaders guide and worksheets for students)

Dear leaders and young women,

Each one of the girls that has come into my home is searching for her worth. I am amazed at their answers when asked what they struggle with the most. The majority of the girls struggle with their body shape, if they are pretty enough, or if they are smart enough.

Have you been where they are? If you could now see yourself at age 16, I think we would see our body with different eyes. It would be wrinkle free with no effects of gravity that are now dragging body parts downward! But the sad truth is you and I still would not be content today if that's all we had to make ourselves feel acceptable to others.

Before we start the study in the book of Titus chapter two, I want you, as young women, to understand where you can find true security and confidence. It helps your heart and your mind to be more open to what God wants to teach you.

Jordan has been coming to Bible study for three years. After doing the study on confidence and security, she said, "I have such a better understanding of who I am in Christ!"

In Titus, you will learn how to be a godly, strong girl. If you live the way God has called you to, there can be much heartache you will avoid. There will be enough hardships in life, and you don't want to add to them.

I am excited this study is in your hands! Commit to make it all the way through! God has so much He wants to teach you as His child. He loves you so much!

LEADER'S GUIDE

Leader, this section will show you how you can use this study.

Thank you for being a godly woman who loves younger women! They want to know the truth! God will send you teachable teens and young adult women. He has for me over a decade.

This Bible study is broken up into **Book One** and **Book Two**. **Book One** teaches the girls who they are in Christ. **Book Two** is a teaching on Titus 2:1-5. God created us male and female. This book goes through the meaning of marriage as a covenant and why God created marriage between a man and a woman, along with a deep study of the word 'love'.

I cannot stress enough that, as a leader, you need to make the time to prepare for each lesson. This is God's Word you are teaching, and it needs to be handled correctly. Pray and ask God to give you wisdom and understanding of what HE is asking you to teach to these vulnerable young women.

As older women, we must never mishandle the Word of God. If you see that you have taught them incorrectly, apologize to the girls and correct what was taught incorrectly. We all make mistakes, and we may have been taught incorrectly in our youth.

As a leader, always remain teachable yourselves. Be careful

not to take a verse out of context. Scripture always backs itself up with other Scripture, and this is why I have the girls look up more than one verse. If a girl asks you a question and you don't know the answer, it's okay to say, "I don't know, let me get back to you next week." Make sure you do! Study! Ask a pastor or someone who knows God's Word, if you can't find the answer. One great site is ***gotquestions.org.*** I use it a lot!

The lessons in this study are ones I have taught girls over the years. Most of them had no one showing them biblical truth. Some are from Christian homes, but most are not. Still, there are a few girls that *are* being taught biblical truths in their homes.

Many of these young women have no concept of what marriage is for or the meaning and beauty of it. I see and witness that they are easy prey to what the culture says about marriage or the lack of it. Some of their homes are displaying the deteriorating erosion of marriage.

The real meaning of love is lost to these young women. "If it feels good to me, it has to be right; it must be love." This is what I hear from some young women. We, as Christian women, have failed what Titus chapter two instructs us to do as mature Christian women.

Age Group
This study was written with around the 13-25 year old age range in mind. As an 'older, mature in Christ' woman leading this study, you may need to change some word verbiage to suit the age group you are leading. For those over 25 years old, I recommend *In the Same Way, Teach... To Lead a Holy Life* study book.

Interesting Perspective

The culture our teens live in is very contrary to what the Bible teaches. Do not be shocked when teens disagree with what you teach that the Bible says or even tell you that you are narrow minded. Just remind them these are God's words, not yours.

Heads up: when a teen gives you their idea of how they had evolved in their thinking, and that you are still in the dark ages, just thank them for their input and sharing how they see things. Yes, I had been told that I was in the dark ages, but thought the same thing about adults when I was a teen. You may say, "Interesting perspective, would you be interested in learning God's perspective and why He says what He does?" Say this kindly and lovingly. As a leader, you want to know where they are spiritually. If you tell them they are wrong, they may never come back.

Trust and PRAY that the Holy Spirit will lead them into God's truth (which they will learn in this study) and show them the lies they believe from our culture today. Let God's Word speak truth to them. Only the Holy Spirit can change them. We, as a leader, do not have to defend God's Word. All we need to do is teach them God's Word as it is written. Please PRAY, PRAY, PRAY for their minds and hearts to be opened!!!

Visual Aids

Included are websites from YouTube videos that go with the lessons. If you find other ones you would like to use, you are free to do so as long as they go with the lesson and tie into the biblical message. *YouTube https://www.youtube.com*

Snack ideas.
If you are doing the study in the evening, snacks such as ice cream and toppings make for a great social time before you begin the study time. Girls love to talk! Or you could have an easy dinner for the girls such as casseroles, tacos, hot dogs, soups and bread, and more along with water or milk to drink. This is also a fun time for the girls to be together. In some way communicate (text) with the girls the night before to remind them and also to get a count of how many can make it. Sometimes ice cream is provided by me, and other times the girls are asked who would like to bring it the next week.

An easy snack for a morning study is sticky buns. Easy recipes at *https://www.pillsbury.com/recipes/grands-monkey-bread* are helpful. Rhodes cinnamon rolls come in a pack of twelve, and you just pop them in the oven. Orange juice or apple juice is a favorite also.

Time and Date
Don't get discouraged if you don't have the same number of girls each week; they have busy schedules if they are in sports.

It's important to have a set day and time for the study. In all the years I have been doing this, the girls like a ritual. I do Monday nights from 5:30 to 7:00. When the study was in the mornings, it was before school from 7:00 to 7:50. I lived a few blocks from school and took the girls that needed a ride. Even if only four girls that can make it on a Monday night, I will meet with the four. They love it! Even one-on-one study with a teen girl is a great thing. Take her for a latte or something!

I started with one girl. If possible, try not to let the group become more than 12 girls. The intimacy is lost, and the quiet ones never talk. Recruit others to do a group.

The meaning of 

When you see this heart, these are the questions the teen girls are to ask themselves and/or to answer. You have my permission to copy the **Question Worksheet Lesson** pages in the back of this book for each chapter as a hand out to keep costs down and then use the book for a leader's guide only. Or you may purchase a book for each girl.

They may share their answers if they feel comfortable. It's easy to get off topic with girls. Reign them in, but let them ask questions also.

When you see this lady, this will be you as the leader. She is there to help you lead. You may read, generalize, or rephrase a question to the girls. If you think of another question that goes with the lesson, it's ok as long as you have a biblical answer. Many times as I lead a study with the girls, we only get halfway, if even, through the lesson. Take your time! Do not rush through it! You do not have to finish a lesson in the half hour or hour that you have with the girls. Just continue where you left off the next time you get together. This Bible study may take a school year to complete.

When you see this flower, this in my personal input. You may read to the girls or maybe have your own personal life experience you would like to share.

to  This means from me to you as a leader. I am with you, encouraging you, and sharing with you what I have learned! What you are doing is so valuable! You are my sister in Christ! Hang in there!

Example:  to  Leader, have the girls look up verses in a different version for other word usages. I let them use their Bible apps on their phones. Encourage them to download it if possible. I am using the NLT (New Living Translation) unless otherwise stated.

When the girls are more comfortable with you and each other, they may open up more. Make sure to let them share life experiences that may fit with what they are learning, but do not let one girl take up all the time. This discourages other girls from coming. There will be girls who love to talk and ones who do not.

If a teen does not want to read Scripture, let her pass. In time, she may. Make sure to stress not to gossip about what others share. I tell them what is said in my front room stays there. If someone wants to share something and you notice it would not be safe, tell the teen to share with you later privately. As a leader, keep in confidence what they tell you. I do tell the girls ahead of time if one talks of them is harming themselves or is talking about someone who is, I need to report it.

Book One

Confidence and Security

In the Same Way, Learn

Having a Teachable Spirit

LESSON 1

INSECURE VS SECURE

Watch Testimony - Stephanie's Awesome Story Of Overcoming Depression, Insecurity, And Thoughts Of Suicide   YouTube https://www.youtube.com

"How can you relate to Stephanie's story?" I asked the group of girls sitting in my living room.

"We all, as high school girls, feel insecure like her, and we lack self-confidence," Megan said.

"Even if we are in a Christian home," Nicole replied.

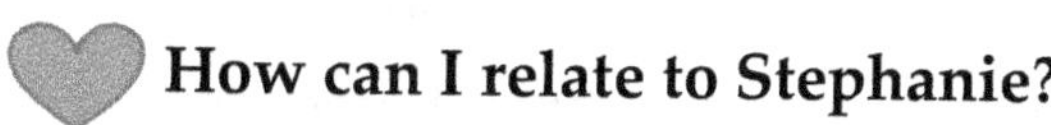

How can I relate to Stephanie?

Do you girls remember when you were carefree? There were no thoughts of how or if you looked attractive to the opposite sex. Do you think your issue with being aware of how you looked to others started when your body started developing? If you were shy before this time in your life, maybe this just added to your shyness.

"I remember not wanting to wear a bra when I got my 'buds'," I shared with the girls.

"Yes, I hated it when I had to start to wear a bra!" the girls chimed together.

"But then my best friend was wearing one, so maybe I should," I told the girls. "When my buds developed, I noticed that boys looked. This hadn't happened before."

If you are comfortable, share when there was a time in your life you started being self-conscious.

Did you know that the Bible mentions a girl's figure?

"The young woman had a beautiful figure and was lovely to look at" (English Standard Version, Esther 2:7b).

From reading this, we see it's not wrong to notice if someone is attractive. Girls, beauty is in the eye of the beholder. What one person thinks is beautiful to look at, someone else may not. But I want you to notice what made others see the attractiveness of Esther.

"Now Esther was winning favor in the eyes of all who saw her" (ESV, Esther 2:15b). Esther had an inner beauty that made her outward beauty shine. Esther had more than her outward beauty. When you read the story of Esther, she is seen as

being different from the other girls. Maybe there was a kindness and softness about her that the other girls did not have. Maybe the other girls gossiping and being catty against each other because they all wanted to be the new queen? Being in high school or college, you know how this can happen! One can be beautiful in appearance until she opens her mouth and ugliness comes out; that can take away from the physical beauty. Agree?

Our relationship with Jesus Christ says a lot about how we present ourselves and how we feel about ourselves.

If someone compliments me, what do I reply back? (Share what you would say).

(Leader, only tell girls this part after they have shared.) **Did you know:**

<u>1. Confident girls</u> say: "Thank you."

<u>2. Conceited girls</u> say: "I know," (then may say, 'I am only kidding,' but trust me, they are not.)

<u>3. Insecure girls</u> say: "You don't mean what you are saying." They cannot accept a compliment. She may say thank you but feels the need to explain her thank you.

I was the latter girl until someone told me, "Elaine, just say thank you when I compliment you."

What I didn't understand was this person was kind to me, and I was rejecting her kindness. I also grew up in a time and cultural background where you did not compliment your children because you might make them conceited. It became clear to me one day when I told my daughter she looked pretty. My grandmother, whom I loved dearly, told me not to say that because my daughter may get a big head. Kindly and respectfully told my grandmother that it's okay to tell your child she looks pretty.

If you are comfortable in your group share. **Which one of the girls am I? 1.Confident, 2. Conceited or 3. Insecure?**

to As a leader, please stress this with your girls' Bible study. "Girls, it's important to have trust in your group. It means you need to have a maturity not to share with your friends who do not attend this Bible study what any of the girls shared about her insecurity. You will only add to this person's insecurity. Tell them, "Let's try and encourage each other!"

Ok girls, let's look at what the Bible says about us and our appearance! How we dress says a lot about if we are feeling secure or insecure and even conceited.

"And I want women to be modest in their appearance. They should wear decent and appropriate clothing and not draw attention to themselves by the way they fix their hair or by wearing gold or pearls or expensive clothes. For women who claim to be devoted to God should make themselves attractive by the good things they do" (New Living Translation, I Timothy 2:9-10).

This verse is not saying it's wrong to wear jewelry or cute clothes or to get our hair done. We just can't let it become an obsession in our lives. The New Living Translation says in verse *9b, "They should wear decent and appropriate clothing and not draw attention to themselves ..."*

"I think when we wear clothes that are not provocative, we are more attractive," Megan said. The rest of the Bible study girls agreed with her. **Do you? Explain.**

Share what I think it means to *draw attention to myself.* Could it be the opposite of decent and appropriate?

Share what I Timothy 2:10 says should draw others to me.

(Leader, if the girls don't know, share with them that it's our behavior and our obedience to God that should draw others to us.)

Share how I can make myself attractive by the things I do or how I present myself.

My dear friend has an hourglass-shaped body. She has struggled with weight all of her life. The world would never call her "attractive," but to me, she screams the word B-E-A-U-T-I-F-U-L! But these are not the things that drew me to love her. She wore the attractiveness of Christ.

What, as a teen girl, draws me to an older woman as a mentor? Is it her body shape, hair, how she dresses? What is it?

How do I want someone to be drawn to me?

Leader, read in Psalm 139:13-18 how He created us and how we are fearfully and wonderfully made. Honestly, girls, do we see ourselves as wonderfully made? Many girls suffer from insecurity. It's one of the enemy's (Satan's) fiery darts he likes to throw at you. We compare ourselves to others and become unsatisfied with how God made us.

YouTube: Knowing My Identity from Youth Bible Study featuring Eric Mason - Bluefish TV https://www.youtube.com

LESSON 2

HOW CAN I OVERCOME INSECURITY?

Who You Are (Inspiring Video) https://www.youtube.com/watch?v=S4s4xpTw3UQ

I am a daughter of the living God! Share who God said you are from this video.

Did you ever think that God sees you as a girl who could change the world? Why or why not?

Let's look up some word meanings.

IN.SE.CURE (adjective) Not confident or assured; uncertain and anxious.

 **Does this insecurity describe me?**

God wants you to be confident in who you are in Him.

CONFIDENT *– The chief Hebrew word translated "confidence" (baTach, and its forms) means, perhaps, radically, "to be open," showing thus what originated the idea of "confidence"; where there was nothing hidden, a person felt safe; it is very frequently rendered "trust".*

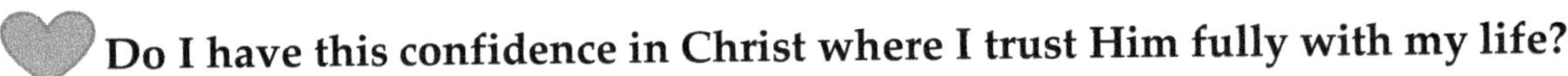

Do I have this confidence in Christ where I trust Him fully with my life?

Did you see that? Insecure is the opposite of confident! So when you say, I am 'just insecure,' you excuse some behavior you don't want to change, or you are telling others that you are not confident! Confidence says that one's destiny is secure in God.

When I am feeling insecure, how can I know what it looks like to attain true security? (Each girl is welcome to have input on any verse read.)

In Jude 24, who can keep me from stumbling?

In John 3:16, what do I have as a believer in Christ?

According to Ephesians 2:8-9, who saved me?

In John 14:6, who is the truth and the way and the life for me?

In I Timothy 6:17, where am I to put my hope?

According to Jeremiah 17:7-8, what does it look like when I trust God?

Read Psalm 9:10. Will God forsake me when I trust in Him?

According to Deuteronomy 31:8, does God ever leave me?

In Lamentations 3:57, what does God say to me?

Read Matthew 6:31-34. Does God know what I need?

According to Philippians 4:19, what will God supply for me?

In Isaiah 26:3, where do I need to put my mind?

to Leader, help the girls summarize what they have learned regarding being secure through reading these Scripture verses. Share how you are learning to be secure in Christ.

When I struggle with feelings of insecurity, (and yes, we still will at times) who do I need to trust?

What happens when I stay in my insecurity and miss the peace of God?

How does this affect the ability to know who I am in Christ?

Who wants to keep me insecure? Read I Peter 5:8 and Ephesians 6:10-18.

What can I do? (James 4:7)

How have you been encouraged of your security in how God made you physically and how He made your personality?

What did you learn in this lesson that you didn't know before regarding how God sees you and knows you?

Watch YouTube: How to Internalize Your Identity in Christ or Your Identity in Christ at https://www.youtube.com.

How can you place your confidence in God and less on what others say or think of you? Do you understand who you are in Christ? We are going to look at what the Bible says about confidence in our next lesson.

Is there a difference between being self-confident and being confident because of who I am in Christ?

How does knowing my identity in Christ makes me confident?

to Leader, if you have time with the girls, have them write down in the back of the book (or you write it down) what they think are the answers to these questions. Then compare them with what God's Word teaches them in the next lesson. When I asked my group of girls these two questions, some of them did not understand the difference between self-confidence compared to confidence in Christ.

LESSON 3

MY IDENTITY IN CHRIST CAN MAKE ME CONFIDENT?

I Am Second - Candace McArthur https://www.youtube.com

How did I see Candace change the way she saw herself after finding her identity in Christ?

Did she ever say that her confidence came from self?

Where did Candace get her confidence? What can I learn from Candace?

Once when I was subbing at school, I had to give a detention to a student who was misbehaving. He looked at me sternly and said, "Do you know who I am?" He proceeded to tell me his full name and how long he and his family had been in the community and church and how important they were. I told him if he was the president of the United States, he was getting a detention. This young man was relying on his self-confidence in who he thought he was to get him out of trouble.

Look at the word self-confident. What is the word in front of confident? Let's look up some verses that talk about self-confidence.

"We rely on what Christ Jesus has done for us. We put no confidence in human effort" (NLT, Philippians 3:3b). This can mean our education, our name, our popularity, or our status in life.

In what ways do I put confidence in my flesh?

"The wise are cautious and avoid danger; fools plunge ahead with reckless confidence" (NLT, Proverbs 14:16). This explains the student I told you about!

What does a fool do?

Do I want this to be me?

Look up and read Galatians 5:17. What are the desires of the flesh and what are the desires of the Spirit?

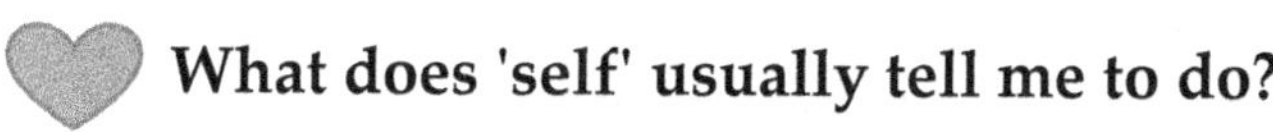

What does 'self' usually tell me to do?

My sinful nature wants me to _________ which is the opposite of what the __________ wants.

What happens when I follow the desires of my sinful nature? (Galatians 5:19-21)

How does following my sinful nature affect my security and confidence?

Now let's look up what the Bible says about confidence.

I love how the Amplified version states II Corinthians 3:4-5, *"Such is the confidence and steadfast reliance and absolute trust that we have through Christ toward God. 5 Not that we are sufficiently qualified in ourselves to claim anything as coming from us,* ***but*** *our sufficiency and qualifications come from God."*

 **In trusting Christ, what can I have according to II Corinthians 3:4?**

Where does this sufficiency and qualification come from according to verse 5b? Did it say anything about 'self '?

What do I see is the difference between my self-confidence and confidence through Christ? Is it different than what I thought it would be?

to Leader, maybe share what you wrote down from the last lesson regarding what the girls thought the difference was between self-confidence and Christ-confidence.

Leader, give the girls a highlighter or pen that they can circle #1 and underline #2 that you will be talking about below.

We are going to look even more into what the Bible tells us regarding how we can have confidence. When we go through these verses, I want you girls to notice two things:

 #1. (Circle) Where does my confidence (*trust)* come from?

#2 (Underline) What am I to do with my confidence?

Ephesians 3:11-12, "*This was his eternal plan, which he carried out through Jesus*

Christ our Lord. Because of Christ and our faith in him, we can now come boldly and confidently into God's presence."

Hebrews 3:6, *"But Christ, as the Son, is in charge of God's entire house. And we are God's house, if we keep our courage and remain confident in our hope in Christ."*

Hebrews 3:14, *"For if we are faithful to the end, trusting God just as firmly as when we first believed, we will share in all that belongs to Christ."*

Hebrews 4:16, *"Let us then with confidence draw near to the throne of grace, that we may receive mercy and find grace to help in time of need."*

I John 4:16-17, "*We know how much God loves us, and we have put our trust in his love. God is love, and all who live in love live in God, and God lives in them. And as we live in God, our love grows more perfect. So we will not be afraid on the day of judgment."*

I John 5:14, *"And we are confident that he hears us whenever we ask for anything that pleases him."*

Hebrews 10: 32b, 35, "*...remember how you remained faithful even though it meant terrible suffering." "So don't throw away this confident trust in the Lord. Remember the great reward it brings you!"*

Hebrews 10:17 and 19, *"Then he says, 'I will never again remember their sins and lawless deeds.'" "And so, dear brothers and sisters, we can boldly enter heaven's Most Holy Place because of the blood of Jesus."*

Share how confidence in Christ makes me more hopeful in struggles I may be facing at school, home, and maybe family?

How am I encouraged in my personal relationship with Christ?

There is one more verse I want to leave with you. I pray and hope, as young women, you see your worth in Christ and how much he adores you!!

"In the fear of the LORD one has strong <u>confidence</u>, and his children will have a ***refuge"*** (English Standard Version, *Proverbs 14:26).*

to to As young adult girls, when you know your identity and confidence is in Christ, you will trust what God's Word teaches you. The rest of the lessons will be focused on what God wants you to learn from 'older' women. This woman can be only a few years older than you or many years older than you, but she must teach God's Word, know God's Word, not change God's Word to fit her or your way of thinking. If someone is teaching you their opinion and it goes against God's Word, RUN!

Book Two

Titus 2:1-5

In the Same Way, Learn

Having a Teachable Spirit

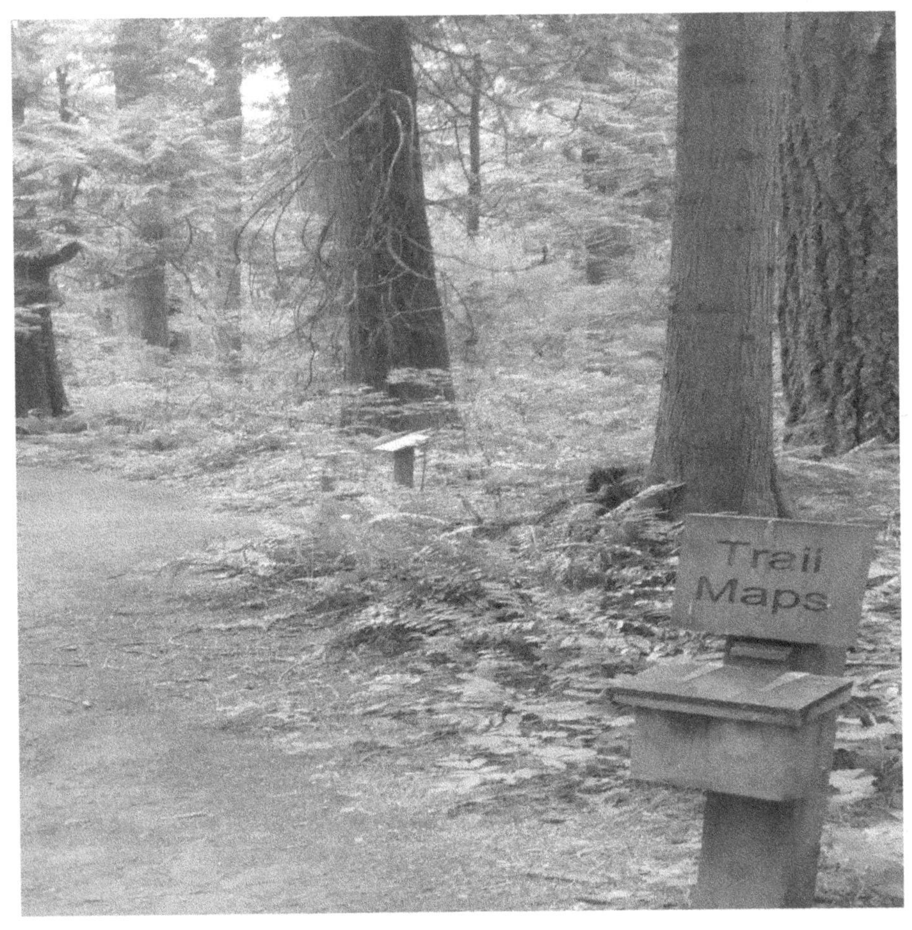

I hope and pray that you have a better understanding of how God sees you. Maybe you are relieved that you do not have to make yourself confident and secure, but God wants to do this in you! And He will.

To remind yourselves, take a marker and write on your bedroom mirror, so you see it every time you look at yourself, "**I am who God says I am.**" I even still need this reminder!

"And 'I will be a Father to you, and you will be my sons and daughters, says the LORD Almighty' " (New International Version, II Corinthians 6:18).

"But as many as received Him, to them He gave the right to become children of God, to those who believe in His name" (New King James Version, John 1:12).

The next part of this study is an exciting journey through Titus 2:1-5. We will go sentence by sentence. Sometimes word by word.

The **bold lettering** represents the topics we will cover.

Be teachable, and you will grow and be more confident!

Pray before each lesson for your heart to receive what the Holy Spirit shows you.

to Here are three different Bible versions of the verses we will be studying. You may copy this page for the girls.

Titus 2:1-5 in the New Living Translation (NLT) reads, *"As for you, Titus, promote the kind of living that reflects **wholesome teaching.** 2 Teach the older men to exercise self-control, to be worthy of respect, and to live wisely. They must have **sound***

faith and be filled with love and patience. *[3] Similarly,* ***teach the older women to live in a way that honors God.*** *They must not slander others or be heavy drinkers. Instead,* ***they should teach others what is good.*** *[4] These older women* ***must train the younger women to love their husbands and their children,*** *[5] to* ***live wisely*** *and* ***be pure,*** *to work in their homes, to do good, and to be* ***submissive*** *to their husbands. Then they will* ***not bring shame on the word of God.***"

Titus 2:1-5 in the English Standard Version (ESV) reads, "**2** *But as for you,* ***teach what accords with sound[a] doctrine.*** *[2] Older men are to be sober-minded, dignified, self-controlled, sound in faith, in love, and in steadfastness. [3] Older women likewise are to* ***be reverent in behavior,*** *not slanderers or slaves to much wine. They are* ***to teach what is good,*** *[4] and so train the* ***young women to love their husbands and children,*** *[5] to be* ***self-controlled, pure,*** *working at home,* ***kind,*** *and* ***submissive*** *to their own husbands, that the word of God may* ***not be reviled.***"

Titus 2:1-5 in the Amplified Bible (AMP) reads, "*Duties of the Older and Younger* **2** *But as for you, teach the things which are in agreement with* ***sound doctrine*** *[which produces men and women of good character whose lifestyle identifies them as true Christians]. [2] Older men are to be temperate, dignified, sensible, sound in faith, in love, in steadfastness [Christlike in character].[3] Older women similarly are to be* ***reverent in their behavior,*** *not malicious gossips nor addicted to much wine,* ***teaching what is right and good,*** *[4] so that they may* ***encourage the young women to tenderly love their husbands and their children,*** *[5] to be* ***sensible, pure,*** *makers of a home [where God is honored],* ***good-natured,*** *being* ***subject*** *to their own husbands, so that the word of God will* ***not be dishonored.***"

Let's dig in!

LESSON 4

KNOWING TRUTH – SOUND DOCTRINE

"But as for you, ***teach*** *what accords with* ***sound doctrine.****" (ESV, Titus 2:1).*

YouTube: DOCTRINE: Video Bible Study for Youth with Teaching from Francis Chan - Bluefish TV https://www.youtube.com **or (and)** *YouTube: Two Scariest Lies in Our World Right Now Francis Chan from Doctrine Youth Study - Bluefish TV https://www.youtube.com/watch*

to These are some of the questions from the video clip. As a leader, you may ask the girls these questions and see what they say for answers.

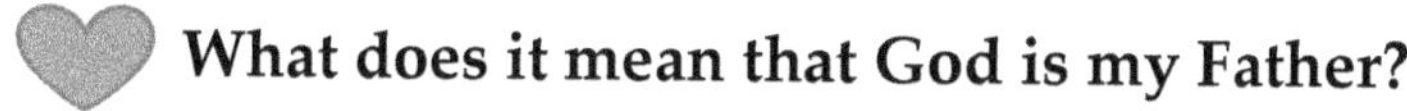
What does it mean that God is my Father?

What am I worshipping?

How do I live out what the Bible says?

What is the most important thing in my life?

Who determines what is right or wrong?

If it doesn't hurt anyone, then why does it matter?

How does God save people?

to to As mature women, before we can teach you, the younger women, we need to have true biblical knowledge. Who better to teach what God's Word has to say than a mature, godly woman who has sound doctrine (teaching). I cannot sufficiently stress that sound doctrine is not always taught today! Some are no longer teaching God's truths, but rather teaching that our culture determines what the Bible means. I see and hear teens are getting confused by the mixed messages they are hearing. They read the Bible then they hear a pastor or teacher say the opposite of what the Bible is saying.

Paul tells Titus in chapter 2 verse 3 what the older women *are to be*. He then instructs us in what we *are to do* and what <u>we *are to teach younger women*</u> and why we are to teach. Even you, as a teen, are older than someone. Timothy in the

Bible was young when he taught God's Word. We are told not to look down on him because of his age. In Titus, we know they are older women because they have husbands and children. These women were told how their behavior should be and I don't think that just applies to an older woman, but all of us.

As an older, mature woman in the Word, I am to teach you sound doctrine.

What is sound doctrine? It's truth; firmness; freedom from error; valid; solid; that cannot be overthrown or refuted. Right; correct, well-founded. Soundness. Correct biblical teaching helps us understand God's will for our lives.

The meaning of Truth:

---

*Sound'ness,n.

Firmness; strength; solidity; truth; as soundness of reasoning or argument, of doctrine or principles. Truth; rectitude; firmness; freedom from error or fallacy; orthodoxy; as soundness of faith. Sound, founded in truth; firm; strong; valid; solid; that cannot be overthrown or refuted; as sound reasoning; a sound reasoning; a sound objection; sound doctrine; sound principle. Right; correct; well founded; free from error; orthodox. II Timothy 1. Let my heart be sound in the statutes. Psalm 119

Girls, what does Mark 9:42 say about the importance of not teaching you false doctrine? *"But if you cause one of these little ones who trusts in me to fall into sin, it would be better for you to have a large millstone tied around your neck and be drowned in the depths of the sea."*

I need to think about this; if I don't have correct biblical doctrine, how can I get God's truth for my life?

Where does God's Word come from?

What is it for?

How can it change me?

Girls, read the verses below and underline where God's Word comes from, circle what it's for and how it can change you.

II Timothy 3:16, *"All Scripture is inspired by God and is useful to teach us what is true and to make us realize what is wrong in our lives. It corrects us when we are wrong and teaches us to do what is right."*

II Peter 1:20-21, *"Above all, you must realize that no prophecy in Scripture ever came from the prophet's own understanding or from human initiative. No, those prophets were moved by the Holy Spirit, and they spoke from God."*

Girls, let's look at some more verses that say what true doctrine (teaching) is and what false doctrine (teaching) is. Underline true teaching and circle false teaching.

II Timothy 4:2-4, *"Preach the word of God. Be prepared, whether the time is favorable or not. Patiently correct, rebuke, and encourage your people with good teaching. For a time is coming when people will no longer listen to sound and wholesome teaching. They will follow their own desires and will look for teachers who will tell them whatever their itching ears want to hear. They will reject the truth and chase after myths."*

II Tim 1:13, *"Hold on to the pattern of wholesome teaching you learned from me—a pattern shaped by the faith and love that you have in Christ Jesus."*

II Timothy 3:5, *"They will act religious, but they will reject the power that could make them godly. Stay away from people like that!"*

I Timothy 1:3-4 *"When I left for Macedonia, I urged you to stay there in Ephesus and stop those whose teaching is contrary to the truth. Don't let them waste their time in endless discussion of myths and spiritual pedigrees. These things only lead to meaningless speculations, which don't help people live a life of faith in God."*

I Timothy 6:3-5, *"Some people may contradict our teaching, but these are the wholesome teachings of the Lord Jesus Christ. These teachings promote a godly life. Anyone who teaches something different is arrogant and lacks understanding. Such a person has an unhealthy desire to quibble over the meaning of words. This stirs up arguments ending in jealousy, division, slander, and evil suspicions. These people always cause trouble. Their minds are corrupt, and they have turned their backs on the truth. To them, a show of godliness is just a way to become wealthy."*

II Peter 1:20-21, *"Above all, you must realize that no prophecy in Scripture ever came from the prophet's own understanding or from human initiative. No, those prophets were moved by the Holy Spirit, and they spoke from God."*

I John 4:1, *"Dear friends, do not believe everyone who claims to speak by the Spirit. You must test them to see if the spirit they have comes from God. For there are many false prophets in the world."*

What is the warning to us, as teachers, in regards to what we present as truth? I Timothy 4:16, "*Keep a close watch on how you live and on your teaching. Stay true to what is right for the sake of your own salvation and the salvation of those who hear you."*

How easily can I be lead astray if my leader doesn't know or understand the authority in which God speaks?

Do you have a better understanding of the importance of sound doctrine?

Galatians 6:12b (NLT) Says, *"they don't want to be persecuted for teaching that the cross alone can save."* **Why are people afraid to teach sound doctrine? Will you be afraid?**

What we believe affects what we do with God's Word. I am so glad you, as young adults, are wanting to study the Word of God for yourselves. *"Work hard so you can present yourself to God and receive his approval. Be a good worker, one who does not need to be ashamed and who correctly explains the word of truth." (NLT, II Timothy 2:15).*

LESSON 5

GODLY LIVING

"Older women likewise are to be ***reverent*** *in behavior,* ***not slanderers or slaves to much wine.*** *They are to teach what is good" (English Standard Version, Titus 2:3).*

This is how the Living Bible translation puts this verse: *"Teach the older women to be quiet and respectful in everything they do."*

YouTube: Dr. Phil Questions a Woman About Her Erratic Behavior https://www.youtube.com

YouTube: Leslie Ludy - True Beauty https://www.youtube.com

to Have the girls watch the two YouTube videos and describe the difference between them.

Which girl/woman is the best example of reverent behavior?

Do you girls want the woman with the erratic behavior as a mentor in your lives or the woman Leslie talks about with the reverent behavior and a desire for God.

Do I think reverent behavior is just for the "older woman"?

The word 'reverent' means an attitude of respect tinged with awe.

"Reverence" To show respect or fear. The root idea of the former is "fear." It is used to express the attitude toward God Himself

---

Did you know you are girls/women of worth? ***When you understand how God sees you, who you are in Him, you will desire be more reverent in your behavior***. You won't want to gossip or get drunk, and you will want to learn and teach what God has shown you about who you are in Him. Teaching those younger than myself has kept me in check and thinking about my personal behavior and habits. I do not want to fail you as young women. I am continually humbled! When leading a Bible study for teen girls and asked them, "What if you found out that I got drunk this past weekend or was gossiping nonstop about everyone?"

"We would not respect you or believe what you taught us," they told me. This comment was the girls' true honesty!

"Oh, God, keep me reverent in all of my behavior! They are watching me!"(And no, I am not in the habit of getting drunk.)

So let's see what God has to say about how He sees us. His Word will show us any behavior that we need to change. When we know how God sees us, this makes us secure and confident. The world cannot give this to us.

to This lesson will help the girls to understand the salvation message. This is an opportunity to ask if any of them have accepted and asked Jesus Christ into their hearts and are ready to give Him their lives and hearts. Pray and listen to the Holy Spirit's timing.

*"I **want you** to know how much I have agonized for **you** and for the church at Laodicea, and for many other believers who have never met me personally. 2 I **want** them to be encouraged and knit together by strong ties of love. I **want** them to have complete confidence that they understand God's mysterious plan, which is Christ himself. 3 In him lie hidden all the treasures of **wisdom** and **knowledge**" (New Living Translation, Colossians 2:1-3).*

What does verse 1 and 2 want for me?

What two treasures are not hidden from me, but for me, in Christ in verse 3?

We have access to wisdom and knowledge when Jesus Christ is our Lord and Savior!

Underline what I am instructed to do when I am in Christ in Colossians 2:6-7.

"Therefore, as you received Christ Jesus the Lord, so walk in him, rooted and built up in him and established in the faith, just as you were taught, abounding in thanksgiving" (English Standard Version, Colossians 2:6-7).

These are the four instructions you should have underlined.

Walk in Him. Learn how He lived his life on this earth.

Be rooted in Him. In trials, our faith is being tested. Trials develop our faith. It's like manure (fertilizer) around the trees; it helps them grow and have strong, deep roots. If a tree could talk, would it say, "Why are you putting that awful, smelly, gross stuff on me?" The gardener reassures the tree it will help it grow into a strong, tall tree. A strong windstorm comes along and the tree, with its roots firmly holding it in place, does not topple over. In our lives, we will have trials. James chapter one tells us this. The trials will produce steadfastness (like a tree). We are being perfected so that we will lack in nothing.

Be built up in Him. We need to know who we are in Christ. We need to know our confidence and security is found only in Him. He is our strength. Learn who God says you are. (Re-read lessons one and two.)

Be established in the faith. Study the Word by yourself and with others.

Which one am I struggling with the most in my life? Share how this verse has encouraged you.

"And you, who were dead in your trespasses and the uncircumcision of your flesh, God made alive together with him, having forgiven us ALL our trespasses" (ESV, Colossians 2:13).

What did Christ Jesus do for me?

You and I did nothing to earn this forgiveness; we are alive because of God!

"But God is so rich in mercy, and he loved us so much, [5] that ***even though we were dead because of our sins****, he gave us life when he raised Christ from the dead. (It is only by God's grace that you have been saved!) [6] For he raised us from the dead along with Christ and* ***seated us with him in the heavenly realms*** *because we are united with* ***Christ Jesus"*** *(New Living Translation, Ephesians 2:4 -6).*

When did God love me?

Where am I seated and *in whom*?

Who saved me?

"For by grace you have been (perfect tense) saved through faith. And this is ***not your own doing****; it is the* ***gift of God*** *not a result of works, so that no one may boast" (English Standard Version, Ephesians 2:8).*

Why can't I save myself?

 to  **Write out John 10:28 and see who gave you eternal life.**

Who has you in His hand?

How secure are you in His hand?

According to I Peter 1:5, what will God do for you in His mighty power?

This salvation is past, present and future. You were saved, you are being saved, and you will be saved until you receive this salvation ready to be revealed in the last time.

 **Do I truly take all this to heart?**

Why do I turn to other 'things' to find my worth?

Do I think what Christ did for me is not enough?

When you don't find your worth in what Christ did for you, you can't give it to the next generation. True or False?

Can you see that when you know your worth in Christ, this spurs you to want to live for Him, live to glorify Him not glorify ourselves (in gossiping, which tears others down)? If we don't understand who we are in Christ, we won't have the urge to live godly, reverent lives.

Do you agree or disagree with that last statement: Why or why not? Share with the group.

Let me give you an example I just experienced.

At a Christmas program, I heard the "Hallelujah" song by my grandson's middle school. Half way through the song, two high school girls sitting in the front aimlessly tried to get the audience to stand up. A few did, including me. I stood because it felt like I was in the presence of our Holy God! I did not know the historical reason why until now of standing during this song. I learned that Handle wrote the song in 1721 and during the time of the monarchy in England, rumor had it King George II stood when he heard the words "King of Kings" and "Lord of Lords". The tradition became when a monarch stood, the common people had to stand out of respect. It was said King George was standing for the greatest monarch, the King of Kings.

You and I live in the presence of the KING daily! Our hearts ought to always have deep respect. It should show in our attitude and actions. Would I gossip if Jesus was standing beside me? No! Perhaps as girls, we are told to be reverent because we are more verbal, and not always careful with what we say. But if anything, we are to be even more reverent in our behavior and words. When we have a reverent respect for God, we will have a reverent respect for others around us.

If you don't have reverence for God, you will not have reverence for others. You will put others down, become slanderers, making others seem lesser than ourselves. You will indulge (don't be slaves to much wine) in what makes me happy, and life becomes all about "me." Self-centeredness is what makes girls/women feel free to put others down.

to **Share as a group maybe how this was done to you, or maybe you have done it to someone. Ask God to help you forgive someone who has put you down, or ask God to help you to apologize to someone you may have put down. Repentance and forgiveness set us free and help us to grow in confidence!**

When we know who we are in Christ, we learn an awesome respect and reverence for how holy God is! We want to become holy as He is Holy. (I will cover this more in a later chapter.)

YouTube; Who am I? | | David Bowden | | Spoken Wordhttps://www.youtube.com (6 minutes)

LESSON 6

RENOUNCE UNGODLINESS

"For the grace of God has appeared, bringing salvation for all people, training us to ***renounce ungodliness*** *and worldly passions, and* ***to live self-controlled, upright, and godly lives in the present age" (ESV, Titus 2:11-12).***

to **Share in your group what you see is ungodliness and worldly passion? Why do we have to be trained to renounce it?**

You Matter | | Spoken Word https://www.youtube.com

Girls, we are going to take a deep look into an Old Testament passage. Did you know when Daniel was your age, he and his teen friends were being held in captivity? You may know the story of Daniel and the lion's den and his friends in the fiery furnace. He stood for God, even though it could have meant death. We complain when our cell phone is dead!

Daniel honored and obeyed God all his life. This passage we are going to look at is Daniel's prayer. It's a prayer you could use also. I do. In Daniel, you will see what you are to do when you see ungodliness and worldly passion.

to **When you read this prayer, I want you to think about why a godly man like Daniel would include himself with the sins of the people.**

Before you start, pray and ask God to show you how He wants to speak to you, then share at the end of this lesson with your group, if you are comfortable.

to In reading this passage, have a highlighter or pen. Every time you see the phrases **we have sinned, we have not listened, we have rebelled, we have not obeyed, and we have done wickedly,** circle or highlight them. When you see the words **us, we,** or **our,** underline them.

Daniel's Prayer for His People **(New Living Translation, Daniel 9: 3-15)**

"So I turned to the Lord God and pleaded with him in prayer and fasting. I also wore rough burlap and sprinkled myself with ashes."

(*When was the last time you wore burlap and ashes? Never I bet! Me neither!*)

"4 I prayed to the LORD my God and confessed: 'O Lord, you are a great and awesome God! You always fulfill your covenant and keep your promises of unfailing love to those who love you and obey your commands. 5 But we have sinned and done wrong. We have rebelled against you and scorned your commands and regulations. 6 We have refused to listen to your servants the prophets, who spoke on your authority to our kings and princes and ancestors and to all the people of the land."

(*Did you see all of the we's! Have you and I ever prayed like that?)*

7 "Lord, you are in the right; but as you see, our faces are covered with shame. This is true of all of us, including the people of Judah and Jerusalem and all Israel, scattered near and far, wherever you have driven us because of our disloyalty to you. 8 O LORD, we and our kings, princes, and ancestors are covered with shame because we have sinned against you. 9 But the Lord our God is merciful and forgiving, even though we have rebelled against him. 10 We have not obeyed the LORD our God, for we have not followed the instructions he gave us through his servants the prophets. 11 All Israel has disobeyed your instruction and turned away, refusing to listen to your voice."

(*Daniel is a great, godly guy, yet he is talking about his shame and sin! Do you and I ever think of our faces covered with shame?)*

"So now the solemn curses and judgments written in the Law of Moses, the servant of God, have been poured down on us because of our sin. 12 You have kept your word and done to us and our rulers exactly as you warned. Never has there been such a disaster as happened in Jerusalem. 13 Every curse written against us in the Law of Moses has come true. Yet we have refused to seek mercy from the LORD our God by turning from our sins and recognizing his truth.14 Therefore, the LORD has brought upon us the disaster he

prepared. The LORD our God was right to do all of these things, for we did not obey him."

(*Is this our culture today? Do we refuse to seek forgiveness and mercy from our sin? Will disaster come upon us? Yikes!*)

15 *"O Lord our God, you brought lasting honor to your name by rescuing your people from Egypt in a great display of power. But we have sinned and are full of wickedness."*

to **What did Daniel acknowledge? Did you notice that he included himself in what they had been doing wrong?** (To me, he was a pretty righteous guy!)

When praying for our nation, have you ever thought of confessing yourself as part of the sin in our nation? Can you say, "We have sinned"?

If we can't acknowledge sin in our lives, sadly nothing will change in us. Please don't evaluate yourself, (meaning through your mindset because our own hearts deceive us), but instead, use God's Word. We can't see our sin sometimes, even when it slaps us in the face.

"Search me, O God, and know my heart! Try me and know my thoughts! And see if there be any grievous way in me, and lead me in the way everlasting!" (English Standard Version, Psalm 139:23-24).

Let's continue with Daniel 9:16-19

 **In verses 16-19, what is Daniel's plea?**

"16 In view of all your faithful mercies, Lord, please turn your furious anger away from
your city Jerusalem, your holy mountain. All the neighboring nations mock Jerusalem
and your people because of our sins and the sins of our ancestors.17 "O our God, hear
your servant's prayer! Listen as I plead. For your own sake, Lord, smile again on your
desolate sanctuary. 18 "O my God, lean down and listen to me. Open your eyes and see
our despair. See how your city—the city that bears your name—lies in ruins. We make
this plea, not because we deserve help, but because of your mercy."

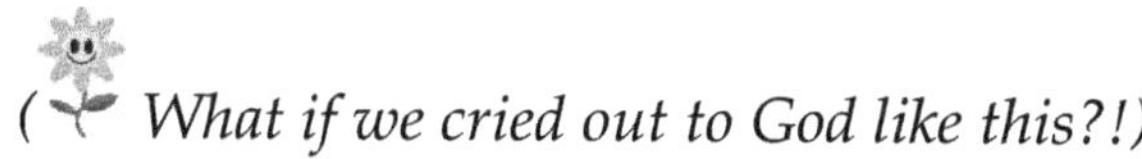
(What if we cried out to God like this?!)

19 "O Lord, hear. O Lord, forgive. O Lord, listen and act! For your own sake, do not
delay, O my God, for your people and your city bear your name."

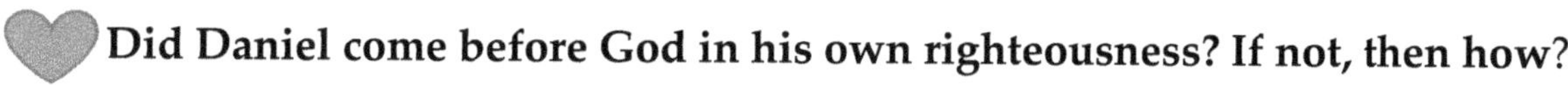
Did Daniel come before God in his own righteousness? If not, then how?

According to Romans 3:10, who is righteous?

In Romans 3:23-25, Who sinned?

What did God do?

How am I made right with God?

This, girls, is how we need to come before God, not in our righteousness but because of God's great mercy and forgiveness. It is then that we learn how to live godly lives. It's ongoing. You and I are being sanctified, meaning, being made holy. We will study more on how to be holy in Lesson 13. We need to be like Daniel, continually crying out to God!

LESSON 7

MEANING OF LOVE – STORGE AND EROS

They are to ***teach what is good,*** *and so train the* ***young women to love.....*** *(ESV, Titus 2:3b-4).*

YouTube: Mark Gungor Teen Edition Sex Dating& Relating 3
www.youtube.com/watch?v=YE7rd89_X6c 1:45:00

How to Tell a Guy You're Saving Sex for Marriage - YouTube
*https://**www.youtube.com** watch?v=LP7K4maLqU0/*

(YouTubes are an option to show, or you could show a part of it that you may see as relevant to this lesson. This YouTube video tells the real truth of the consequences of sex outside of God's plan that our youth are not hearing. The youth I showed it to loved it! They wondered why no one is telling this truth).

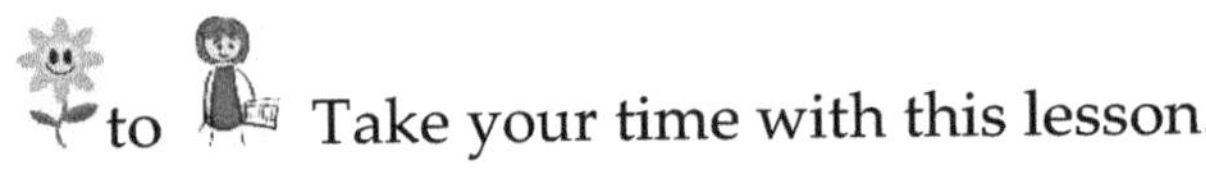

to Take your time with this lesson.

I pray with the lesson you have just completed, the girls you are leading have a better understanding of how much God loves them and a better understanding of His forgiveness when we repent. In this next part of Titus, we are going to dig deeper into the meaning of love. Please, leaders, take your time with this lesson. It's okay if it takes a couple of weeks. It may brings up many discussions with the girls you are teaching. You want them to understand when we repent and receive forgiveness of our sin, we are set free. We don't want to withhold this wonderful news from anyone.

to **Before we start, I want you to write down or talk about what you think the word 'love' means. When we are done with the lesson on love, I want you to look at what you wrote down and see if it's the same as what you are about to learn.**

"They are to ***teach what is good,*** *and so train the* ***young women to love ..."*** *(ESV, Titus 2:3b-4a).* In this one sentence, we are told to teach what is right and good and so train others to love. Why? I think, as girls, God has given us a desire to be loved, where men feel the need to be respected.

We tend to throw around the word 'love' without even thinking. I love my cat, I love food, and I love it when it rains. I love my boyfriend. I love my best friend. Did you know each of these types of love has a different meaning? Do you need to know the meaning of the word love? Yes! So many young women and young girls think they are in love when it may be just an infatuation.

Do you ever hear the phrase, 'They are in love, how can it be wrong?' I hear this a lot from young adults. I used to say it myself when I was a teen. But what I find sad is girls growing up into young women with the same train of thought. They let their feelings lead them into relationships that are sometimes destructive. "Let your heart lead you" or "Go where your heart leads you" are very famous sayings. My own heart gets me into real trouble at times! Does yours? I am continually praying, "God create in me a clean heart!" I am going to follow God's Word. The Word of God gives much better instructions on how to live my life than my heart does.

We are going to study the meaning of the word 'love' and what God's Word has to say about it, not our hearts.

There are four Greek words for love: **storge, eros, phileo, and agape**. We will look at how the meaning of love gets distorted and the biblical meaning of these words.

The first word we are going to look at is **STORGE.**

STORGE (ˈstɔːgɪ) *n* natural or instinctual affection, as of a parent for a child

---

God created us to have a natural affection, an obligation to treat others kindly.

 **What does this love look like in Romans 12:9-10?**

Natural affection is the feeling for a wife, husband, child, and sibling. It is the abiding feeling within a man ("man" meaning male or female) that rests on something close to him which he feels good about inside himself. This kind of love is not passionate or erotic. It's a familiar love.

 to **Can you think of some examples of storge love?**

When this kind of love is perverted or lost, what happens to humans in Romans 1:28-32 and II Timothy 3:3?

 Opposite of storge in Greek is *Astorgos* which means "without love, devoid of affection, without affection to kindred, hard-hearted, and unfeeling.

Why would someone be without love?

to **Who or what do you think has a hold of this person's heart? (Mark 7:21)**

EROS

We are going to take more time and study on this word. There is a lot of confusion as to the meaning of this love. The definition of eros is portrayed in the Old Testament book, *Song of Solomon*. This word is not used in the New

---

EROS described the healthy, common expressions of physical love. In the Scriptures, *eros* primarily refers to those expressions of love carried out between a husband and wife." (Sam O'Neal)

Testament. Eros is the physical, sensual intimacy between a husband and wife. Eros is a word used to express sexual love or feeling of arousal between two people. God created sexual intimacy for marriage. God made us sexual beings. Therefore, you will have feelings as long as you live and breathe.

What you feel when you are close to a boy or kiss him is normal. It's part of our makeup as humans in how God created us. But our feelings need to be held in check in life. If feelings control us, we would be a mess! If I ate every time something looked yummy, what would happen? If I said every thought, what would happen? If, as a married woman, I kissed every guy I thought was cute, what would happen? Yeah, nothing good! Girls, just as it's wrong for me, as a married woman, to be sexually intimate with someone other than my husband, it's wrong for you to be sexually intimate with someone you are not married to. There will be consequences for you and me.

Let's look at what the Word teaches us on how to handle the physical feelings outside of marriage. This is where, as older women, we teach what is right and good.

 **This type of love needs proper boundaries. What are these boundaries in:**

I Corinthians 7:8-9?

Hebrews 13:4

I Corinthians 7:5

"Eros love is part of God's design, a gift of his goodness for procreation and

enjoyment. Sex, as God intended it, is a source of delight and a beautiful blessing between a man and a woman who are married to each other." (Sam O'Neal)

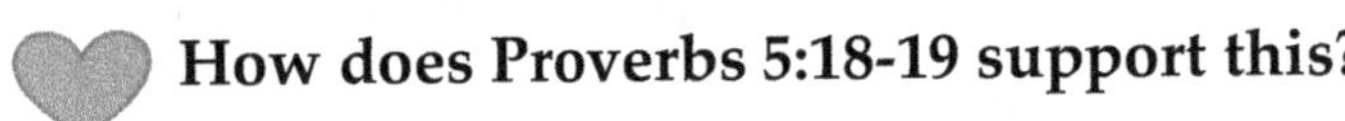

How does Proverbs 5:18-19 support this?

What do I see in the world that has happened when eros is outside of God's plan?

Eros is a love of passion erotic that absorbs itself into the mind and emotions based on body chemistry (with no boundaries). This love is self-satisfaction. It is directed toward another to use them for self-gratification; it has itself in mind. "I love you because you make **me** happy." This love doesn't care about consequences because it is self-seeking. It's only the characteristics of the other person which please **you.** If this feeling of 'happy' ceases to exist, love will be gone. Eros looks for what **it** can receive. ***It gives only to receive.*** If it fails to get what it wants, bitterness and resentment will set in our hearts. Marriages do not last if built on this type of love. Typically, this is the teen love that is lost for genuine love. Any sex before marriage, outside of God's plan for marriage, is eros love. ***It's conditional and depends on being attracted to the other person. It causes affairs in marriage. It's a very self-centered love.***

Is this the kind of love I want, love that only gives to receive?

If I give myself sexually to a guy who says he loves me and then the next day

or so I see him with someone else, what do I think will happen to my heart?

A guy gives love to get sex, a girl gives sex to get love. True or False?

Why do I think marriage will not last if it's built on eros love?

Do I want the guy I am going to marry to love me unconditionally?

With eros love, what happens when a guy no longer finds me attractive?

What security do I have in a relationship if I move in with my boyfriend? Are we honestly committed to each other?

Put aside what the world has been telling you if you disagree with me at this point. When sin entered the world, so did diseases and death. We looked up verses on the boundaries of eros love. We see God loves us so much! He created our bodies, and He knows how they work more than we do. He knows what will happen to us if we have eros outside of His boundaries. We see it, but ignore the consequences of it and continue to call it 'love.' Please hear me out on this. I want to save you a lot of hurts emotionally and physically!

When a man and woman wait until they get married to have sex, save themselves sexually for each other, there is no worry of sexually transmitted diseases. True **agape** love is always looking out for your loved one. You also don't get diseases or die from this kind of sex. Remember this.

Side note: If you, like me, didn't really understand that true love waits and lost your virginity before marriage, I want to encourage you at this point. We can't go back and undo what we did. I want you to know that we serve a merciful God and a forgiving God of second chances. When I really understood that sex before marriage was wrong and God convicted me, He did not condemn me. I repented and He forgave me. Is abstinence easy? No. Realistic? Yes. But only when we believe God's truth. A good verse to memorize is I Corinthians 10:13, *"No temptation has overtaken you except what is common to mankind. And God is faithful; he will not let you be tempted beyond what you can bear. But when you are tempted, he will also provide a way out so that you can endure it."*

When we have erotic (eros) sex outside the boundaries of marriage, we are always looking for our pleasure. We take great risk in passing diseases to another person because our pleasure comes first. You learn in health class at school that when you have multiple partners, you are at great risk of getting a sexually transmitted disease. (Do schools still teach this?) Teens I know have contracted a disease due to unbridled passion outside of marriage and now have to fight it the rest of their lives. They now have to share this with the person they were going to marry and risk giving them the disease.

What does Romans 1:27 tell me about what happens when I believe I can go outside the boundaries of God's Word and then encourage others to do the same?

Why, as a Christian, would I want others to receive a due penalty? Roman 1: 32 tells us it's the death penalty. Doesn't this make your heart sad?

Read Romans 1:24-32 in full context. How am I sending others to their death by justifying their sin?

Are there any Scriptures that support a sexual relationship that is not just between a married man and woman? Does this matter?

Is man wiser than God in how He created our bodies to function?

How do I define what sin is if I don't believe what God says?

If I decide myself what I and others can do sexually and we have no moral law,

what could happen? Could little children be sexually abused?

to **Read Leviticus 18:6-23 and see what would be acceptable if we did not believe God's Word. (Where the verse says "do not" replace with "I think they can because I love them and accept them as they are.")**

II Corinthians 11:2-4, how can my pure devotion to Christ be led astray when I listen to a false teaching that is not in God's Word?

I am so proud of you all for doing this study! It's hard work. I pray you continue! Keep on being teachable! Listen to what the Holy Spirit is teaching you. Beware of what the world is teaching you.

God ordained marriage for a man and a woman, not man to another man or women to women. I innocently used to believe if you were a Christian, you understood and knew why God created sex and for whom. I still believe that God's Word was the same yesterday, today, and tomorrow. Today, many Christians seem to be looking at society and what seems right to man, rather than God's Word. Could it be because our belief in God's Word is being challenged legally and we are seeing the cost of following Jesus Christ? I know I am responsible for telling the truth of God's Word, even if I share what the Bible says and it is not received or if I end up in jail for teaching on passages in the Bible which the world finds offensive.

LESSON 8

MY HEART

"The seed of every sin is in every heart." (Quote by John Owen)

Let's do our own heart cleaning before we go on to Phileo and Agape love. Also, remember Daniel's prayer in Lesson 6?

When we recognize our brokenness with deep humility, any personal righteousness about our sin should embarrass and anger us. We are all born with a sin nature giving us a commonality with all kinds of sinners. When you teach or talk about sexual sins (or any sin) in your neighbor's eye, you need to see it through the log of your depravity. You need to be more angered by your own sin than what sin is in someone else's heart. Your heart needs to overflow at how God has forgiven you. But if you are so focused on other people's sin, you are out of touch with the gospel. Refusing to acknowledge your brokenness keeps you outside of God's grace. When you and I become blind to our own sin. But, we cannot push away people who are being deceived about their sexual lifestyle, or any sin. If we do, we keep them away from the gift of eternal life.

 **According to Matthew 7:2-5, who has the speck and who has the log?**

What am I to do first? Why?

After I do my part, then what can I do?

In Romans 3:23, what do I read that we all have done and fallen short of?

How does learning about planks and logs change how you may see yourself and others?

to When you go through the next passages with the girls, some may not know what some of the words mean. I talked to a 23 year old who did not know what dissension was. She told me her generation does not use some of these words. Let them use their phones to look up word meanings.

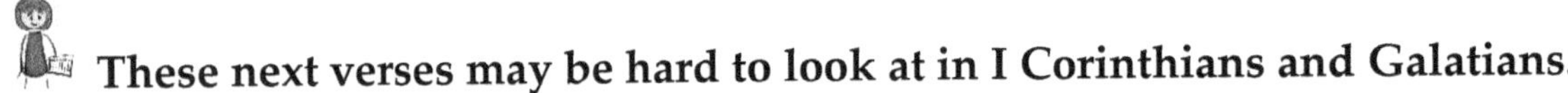

These next verses may be hard to look at in I Corinthians and Galatians.

Underline each sin that we are capable of because we are born with a sin nature. Yes, we are *born* that way. We each struggle with a different tendency of sin. I sure had my struggles with the sins listed below!

"9Don't you realize that those who do wrong will not inherit the Kingdom of God? Don't fool yourselves. Those who indulge in sexual sin, or who worship idols, or commit adultery, or are male prostitutes, or practice homosexuality, [10] or are thieves, or greedy people, or drunkards, or are abusive, or cheat people—none of these will inherit the Kingdom of God.[11] Some of you were once like that. But you were cleansed; you were made holy; you were made right with God by calling on the name of the Lord Jesus Christ and by the Spirit of our God." (New Living Translation, I Corinthians 6:9-11).

"When you follow the desires of your sinful nature, the results are very clear: sexual immorality, impurity, lustful pleasure, idolatry, sorcery, hostility, quarreling, jealousy, outbursts of anger, selfish ambition, dissension, division, envy, drunkenness, wild parties, and other sins like these. Let me tell you again, as I have before, that anyone living that sort of life will not inherit the Kingdom of God" (NLT, Galatians 5:19-21).

What have those who belong to Christ Jesus done? *(Galatians 5:24) (This is what I do with my struggles with sin!)*

A lot of sins are covered in these verses. Other Scriptures give even more details of sin. The point is, we ALL sin.

In I Corinthians 6:9-10, what was I before I believed? Do I see that none of us are without sin?

How is verse 11 full of hope in I Corinthians 6?

What happens to my old life in II Corinthians 5:17?

When you and I justify someone's sin because I and others think we are loving them, what does I Corinthians 6:10 tell me we are withholding from them?

Verse 10b says *"none of these will inherit the Kingdom of God"*.

Who are the none?

Do I believe what God is saying? Or do I believe my culture?

How is it loving to withhold the truth of God's Word from those who are perishing?

What does God desire when I sin? (II Peter 3:9)

How does John 3:16 make this possible?

In John 3:20, what keeps me and others from eternal life?

I need to ask you a hard question. Do you believe what God says or what culture is saying about sex? Would you be ok with the man you marry to be sleeping around with other women if he had this sin tendency? Can we pick and choose which sins and sexual sins are acceptable and find ways to excuse and justify when God's Word is so clear?

Are you willing to be called names like bigot or basher, be looked down upon, lose a job or a friend, be misunderstood, and told you hate because you believe God's Word? You know you don't have any hate in your heart, and no matter how gentle, how loving, and how kind you can be in teaching the true Word of God, they see you as hateful. Jesus was hated.

Do you and I believe what Jesus said? "If you want to follow me, take up your cross." What happened to Jesus when he went against culture? Or will you and I be like others and drop our cross and say, "It's hard to follow Jesus. I care more about what my friends think of me."

Girls, the last days will even be harder for us as believers. Read Matthew 24. Many are being killed for their faith right now. Are we a little or a lot spoiled here? Remain teachable even at this point if you don't agree with what God's Word says. (It's not my word, so talk to God about what you don't agree with.) I wonder, would you and I tell God He does not love people?

Eternity is forever; this earth is a short time. I would rather be mocked on this earth and hated than be separated from God forever. Oh, how I pray with tears that you would not want to be separated from God! Let's keep learning what God wants us to know! Pray for our hearts to receive God's truth!

Ok, I have one more verse I want you to look at! I know this is a long lesson, but it's important!

 **Use these verses to answer the following questions.**

"Run from sexual sin! No other sin so clearly affects the body as this one does. For sexual immorality is a sin against your own body. [19] *Don't you realize that your body is the temple of the Holy Spirit, who lives in you and was given to you by God? You do not belong to yourself,* [20] *for God bought you with a high price. So you must honor God with your body."* (NLT, I Corinthians 6:18-20)

(Verse 18b) Sexual immorality is a sin __________your own___________.
(Verse 19) My body is the ______ of the _____ ________

Who lives in me?

Who gave me my body?

Do I have the right to do with my body whatever I want? (Verse 19)

Who do I belong to, who bought me, and who lives in me?

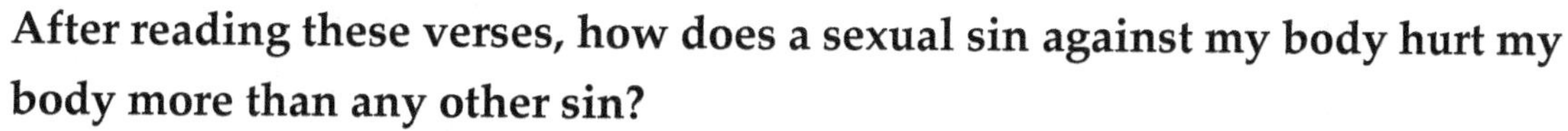

After reading these verses, how does a sexual sin against my body hurt my body more than any other sin?

I will reword it this way, how can sexual immorality consume your flesh and your body and your heart and your mind more destructively than any other sin?

According to I Peter 1:15-16, how am I to live?

What does Roman 12:1-2 say that my body is to be?

Jesus came to die for all our sins and temptations. If He hadn't, we would be doomed!

If some still struggle with what God says about homosexuality, these are encouraging YouTube video.

Homosexuality Was My Identity
https://www.youtube.com/watch?v=K8a5I0yv0Dw (about 7 minutes)

"Love Revived" A Christian Apology to the LGBT Community
https://www.youtube.com/watch?v=oKk3or5MXQ0
(This YouTube goes well with Matthew 7:5 when we think someone's else's sin is greater than my own and may feel they deserve my judgement).

Messy Grace – Caleb Kaltenbach
messygracebook.com/
(How a Pastor with Gay Parents Learned to Love Others Without Sacrificing Conviction).

LESSON 9

MEANING OF LOVE - PHILEO AND AGAPE

PHILEO *To love, to approve of, to like, sanction, to treat affectionately or kindly, to welcome, befriend, to show signs of love, to kiss, to be fond of doing.*
https://www.blueletterbible.org/lang/lexicon/lexicon.cfm?t=KJV&strongs=G5368

Optional: Sex and Dating Advice for Teenagers - Mark Gungor
https://www.youtube.com

What is agape love? https://www.youtube.com/watch?v=W3Yk-c9_PtQ&t=12s

In this lesson, we are going to finish up with the last two meanings of the word 'love'.

Phileo is a companionable love, rich in emotion, brotherly love. It is a friendship-type love and non-sexual. It's not a love toward our enemies. It is warmth and affection toward another person. I think of this love when I watch my grandkids play or when they say something that warms my heart. I smile, remembering all the years I had a Bible study for teen girls in my front room, sitting in front of my fireplace, eating cinnamon rolls. I have phileo love for them and you!

We don't have this toward someone who treats us badly or hurts us. When we learn agape love, we may experience phileo toward difficult people. At times this love can be shallow and conditional. It can depend on how others treat us. Let's see what God's Word says about this love!

 **What do these verses tell me about phileo love?**

I Thessalonians 4:9

I Samuel 18:1-3

Romans 12:10

Hebrews 13:1

In Jude 1b, what name does Jude have for those who are called?

Phileo is the love we have for fellow believers. Phileo love involves giving as well as receiving. This love is higher than eros love because it's about **our** happiness rather than **my** happiness. This love is called out of one's heart by qualities in another. BUT this love can fail when significantly strained; it can collapse in a crisis. This love is still conditional and natural.

 **AGAPE, our final love, and most important one.**

AGAPE *Love (Noun) selfless love of one person to another without sexual implications (especially love that is spiritual in nature). Agape love involves faithfulness, commitment, and an act of the will. It is distinguished from the other types of love by its lofty moral mature and strong character. Agape love is beautifully described in I Corinthians 13."*

Word Study: Agape - "Love" https://www.youtube.com/watch?v=slyevQ1LW7A

Agape is the love God commands us to have toward each other including those who hurt us, are rude to us, hate us, people we clash with as far as personalities and those who persecute us because of our faith. **Read Matthew 5:44.**

Agape can't be earned. It delights in giving. It keeps on loving when the loved one is unresponsive, unkind, unlovable, and unworthy. It's unconditional. It is a consuming passion for the well-being of others. It would do nothing to jeopardize the other person.

In John 3:16, what did God do for me while I was still unresponsive, unkind, unlovable, and unworthy?

 **Some contrasts between agape and phileo are as follows:**

Phileo	Agape
Natural	Learned
Emotional	choose to love
Discriminatory	Non-discriminatory
Conditional	Unconditional
Pleasure	Preciousness
Delight	Esteem
Liking	Prizing
Because of	In spite of
Fails	Never fails

Agape love is beautifully described in I Corinthians 13. Write down what love.

IS -

IS NOT -

We can only agape love others when we see them through God's eyes. This love has nothing to do with feelings, unlike the other meanings of love. Agape is a will of the mind. It is obedience to God. It's an action word.

What is agape love? Write out the following Scriptures.

John 17:26

Romans 5:5, 8

Galatians 5:22

In John 13:35 and I John 3:16, what does this love look like for me?

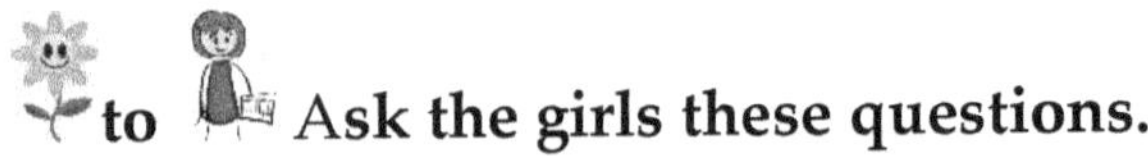

to Ask the girls these questions.

Girls, summarize what you learned about the word 'love'. How is it different than what you wrote on page 44 what you thought the word love meant?

What kind of love should you have toward my spouse one day? Toward your children? Family? Friends?

How has the study of the word 'love' helped you understand God's love for you more?

Do you see how God's love is unconditional and your love is conditional?

Lord Jesus, help us to love one another as you love us! Help us to see others through Your eyes and how much You love us all, no more no less! We are all made in the image of God. Help us to tell Your truths, and not to cast others off as hopeless. You loved the woman caught in adultery, while others condemned her. You were an advocate for her. You forgave her and told her to go sin no more. It was the same with the woman at the well. The disciples couldn't believe You would even talk to someone like her. But you saw her worth! And many believed because of her testimony. Help us to love as You love!

LESSON 10

PATTERN FOR MARRIAGE

Optional: Sex and Dating Advice for Teenagers - Mark Gungor
https://www.youtube.com

What is love spoken word sex before marriage you ask I answered by
Clayton Jennings
https://www.bing.com/videos/search?q=what+is+love+spoken+word+sex+before+marriage+you+ask+I+answered&go=Search&qs=ds&form=QBVDMH *(9 minutes very good!)*

I am excited to teach you this lesson with your leader! I am eager to teach what God's plan was and always will be for marriage. The world is changing the meaning, and so many people are being lied to and believe what the world is teaching them. This is why we see so many families torn apart with no idea of how to make a commitment. I am ready! Let's dig in and learn!

Let's go back to Genesis 2:21-25 and look at the first wedding. It's not like today. Adam and Eve didn't have to get a marriage license or send out an invitation. There was no one to invite! We have pastors or judges officiate our weddings; Adam and Eve had God. God is the inventor of marriage, not man.

Read Genesis 2:18-25. What is the first thing God said about the man?

All the animals had mates, but no mate was found for Adam. Verse 20 says, *"There was not a* ***helper*** *fit for him."*

"helper *(Hb. 'ezer) is one who supplies strength in the area that is lacking in "the helped." This term does not imply that the helper is either stronger or weaker than the one helped."*

God puts Adam to sleep. What does God take out of the man? (Genesis 2:21)

What was fashioned from the rib? (Genesis 2:22)

Go back to Genesis 2:7. How did God make Adam?

to Because I love this passage in Genesis, I am going to go down a short rabbit trail. I want you to know this for yourself and to be able to teach it. God has His hands on us! He breathes life into us! We have no right to take it from any person, in or out of the womb.

 **What did God breathe into Adam?**

(This breath is spiritual, mental, and physical into the one to bear His image!)

Read and write out Job 33:4

How did God create animals, fish, and birds? (Genesis 2:19)

What did God use to create man and woman?

(He used dust and breath and His hands. Did you see this?)

 ***Physical Breath***

 **Is God still forming us today and breathing life into us?** (Psalm 139:13-14)

Spiritual Breath

"Humans can reproduce only human life, but the Holy Spirit gives birth to spiritual life.[a] 7 So don't be surprised when I say, 'You[b] must be born again.' 8 The wind blows wherever it wants. Just as you can hear the wind but can't tell where it comes from or where it is going, so you can't explain how people are born of the Spirit" (NLT, John 3:6-8).

How is spiritual breath different than physical breath?

Did you enjoyed that little trail? Back to Adam and Eve and marriage! It's important for you to look up how Adam was created versus how God made Eve. It has to do with the covenant of marriage. We are going to study this shortly. Just hang in there with me as we go through this passage on the first wedding.

Read Genesis 2:23. Adam is awake. What does he say?

The first wedding was in a beautiful garden! (And man thinks he invented outdoor weddings.)

In Genesis 2:24, what is the standard of how all future marriages are defined?

In Matthew 19:4-6, how did God make Adam and Eve?

What shall the two become?

What are they not?

This, girls, is the pattern for marriage that we are to teach. It's exciting! God established this pattern in the Old Testament and reaffirmed it in the New Testament. His plans for a man and a woman to become one flesh has not changed!

to to What God ordained from the beginning of time is set in stone. There are no Scriptures that change the meaning of marriage of one man to one woman. None.

In Romans 8:7, why is the world changing what God has ordained for marriage?

The Hebrew word for "wife" is gender specific and means woman.

Strong's Concordance Ishshah – woman, wife, female

We need to ask ourselves if we have a mind that is hostile toward God. Have you, like me, had a hostile mind when you want to see things your way? Oh, Lord, forgive us when we do! Yes, in spite of what the world is trying to tell us, we do have a gender, it's either male or female. Who are you going to believe: the everlasting God who created you or a mere man, who is like a flower - here today, gone tomorrow?

The Bible in Genesis shows us that Eve came from Adam's side. She was flesh of his flesh. The two became *one flesh.* God was showing us the essential of marriage and that it's meant to be forever, till death do us part. Divorce is so painful because it is tearing away this *one flesh.*

to to When teaching this lesson to teen girls, I take two pieces of paper and glue them together to make a visual picture of *one flesh*. I then try to pull the pieces of paper apart, and it's a torn mess. Each piece, even though torn, has pieces of the other paper stuck to it. Why? The *one flesh* means glued, stuck together for eternity. No man can separate it. Remember, till death do us part.

Marriage is the commitment we make, a covenant before God. When the girls of divorced parents are asked if they could have their biological parents together, would they? They ALL say, "Yes!" I explain to them that this is why God hates (yet permits under certain circumstances) divorce; it hurts the kids and families, shredding them like the paper I tore. It causes so much pain. I hear parents say, "Oh, the kids will be fine. They will get over it." No, they won't. Women in their 60s still hurt from their parents' divorce.

Sticking it out in some marriages can even be more painful and may not be possible. I am just telling you the deep yearning voiced from teens that just want their first parents back together and loving each other! I remind them we live in a sin-filled world and there are no perfect families out there. Mine included.

to  As mature Christian women, we need to teach the younger women how to find a godly mate, to learn to wait and not to settle for whatever is out there. Teach them to know who they are in Christ first and the guy they are dating to know who he is in Christ first. Maybe this will cut down the divorce rate among Christians.

As mature women, we need to be teaching these young women what to look for in a mate. They need to know how to see warning signs. If girls are sexually active before marriage, they will become blind and ignore all the flashing neon lights that are blaring at them! Their minds tell them it will get better once they are married. Those of us who are married know that is the biggest lie we can tell ourselves. What you see is what you get! Past behavior predicts future behavior UNLESS God gets a hold of their hearts, and they submit their lives to Him. Until then, DON'T marry the guy! I am also talking to the women who are no longer teenagers and looking to remarry or be married for the first time.

CHAPTER 11

MARRIAGE AS A COVENANT. WHAT?

"And so train the young women ***to love their husbands and children."*** *(English Standard Version, Titus 2:4)*

YouTube: Covenant vs Contract in Marriage https://www.youtube.com

Or Strictest Marriage Contract Ever? – Covenant Marriage https;//www.youtube.com

Or The Covenant of Marriage https://www.youtube.com

Covenant is a word you do not hear too much today, especially when it comes to marriage. I never knew about this when I got married. Before we start, let's look at the meaning of this word.

What is a covenant? Have you ever heard of this word referring to marriage?

Ask the girls these questions and see if at the end of the lesson they have a better understanding of covenant.

In previous lessons, we looked at God's pattern for marriage in light of the meanings of the definitions of love. I am going to take you deeper into the definition of marriage.

The first mention of marriage being a covenant is found in Malachi 2:14, 15, *"Because the LORD was witness between you and the wife of your youth, to whom you have been faithless, though she is your companion and your wife by* ***covenant.*** *Did he not make them one, with a portion of the Spirit in their union? And what was the one God seeking?* ***Godly offspring***. *So guard yourselves in your spirit, and let none of you be faithless to the wife of your youth."*

What does this passage teach about marriage and children?

The one kind of covenant that's never broken is when God makes a covenant with us. This is an unconditional covenant. God always keeps His Word. All the other covenants that are broken are made from man to man or man to God. These are conditional covenants, broken when someone doesn't keep their word.

When a covenant was made in the Bible, there was an exchange of something or a sign (for instance, a rainbow promised by God not to flood the whole earth again). A shoe handed to a person or a **cutting** of something represented a covenant. **Blood was shed in covenants**. A mingling of blood. In the Old Covenant, the Israelites had to sacrifice animals for the forgiveness of their sins. Hebrews 10:4 tells us this never took away sin. The Old Covenant was a picture of the New Covenant in Jesus' death on the cross. *"We have been made holy through the sacrifice of the body of Jesus Christ* ***once for all****"* (New International Version, Hebrews 10:10). *(The Hebrew word Berith means "a cutting")* *http://www.biblestudytools.com/dictionary/covenant*

to **What did Christ shed for you on the cross? Why? (I John 1:7 and Romans 5:9)**

Marriage is a covenant. There is a shedding of blood when two become one. When God created our bodies, He placed in women **a hymen**.

The hymen is a membrane that surrounds or partially covers the external vaginal opening. It forms part of the vulva, or external genitalia, and is similar in structure to the vagina."

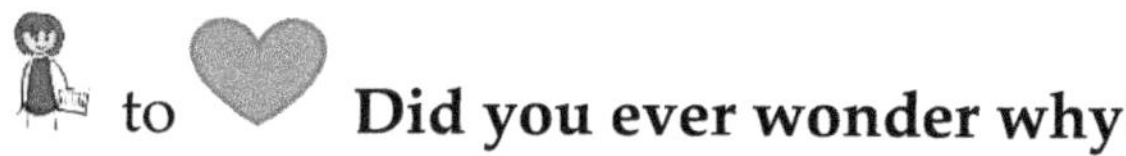

Did you ever wonder why?

When a married couple comes together for the first time sexually, the hymen breaks, and there is the shedding of blood, a sign of a covenant. Of course, with remarriage this does not happen, but God is revealing to us how seriously He takes marriage and the promise a couple who marries is making. It is a covenant relationship.

to **Look up Ephesians 5:31. What do man and woman become when they leave their father and their mother?**

When God spoke of two people being joined as one, He was referring to something we're only beginning to understand in a real, physiological way. When two people are intimate, the hypothalamus in the brain releases chemicals that induce feelings of attachment and trust. Having sex outside of marriage results in a person forming an attachment and trusting someone with whom he or she does not have a committed relationship. The definition of trust in the mind deteriorates. To have that kind of link with someone without the security of working together toward God is dangerous. Two individuals who are—even mildly—physiologically obsessed with each other but not committed to growing in God as a couple can be torn from God and His plans for them."
http:www.gotquestions.org/.html old covenant

---

to There are many reasons God ordained marriage. Let's look up some verses. (Some you have already looked up).

Genesis 2:18

Malachi 2:13-16

What is God seeking? (Verse 15)

Why does God want us to be faithful to our spouses? (Verse 16)

What are we protected from in marriage? (I Corinthians 7:2)

What does Proverbs 18:22 say about marriage? (If you have a Message version, look it up in there and other versions.)

Marriage is a picture of Christ and His Church

YouTube Bride Of Christ Surrender!! Inspirational Christian Video!!
https://www.youtube.com

 **Read Ephesians 5:25-26 and answer the following questions.**

 **What did Christ do for His bride?**

How is this an example of what husbands are to do?

to **For wives, when you become one, you are not off the hook. What are we to do according to Ephesians 5:22-24?**

When will the bride of Christ, the Church (us) be united with Him? (ESV, Revelation 19:7-9, 21:1-2 and 22:20)

Can you remain unmarried? (I Corinthians 7:7-9, 32-35, 37)

When should you be married? (I Corinthians 7:1-2)

Do you now have a better understanding of the covenant of marriage? Share what you learned. How is it different than when I first asked you what a covenant was?

Why is it important for you to understand why God ordained marriage?

Do you see why Satan is out to destroy the meaning of marriage and family? What can you do as one person to stop Satan's plan for you? God has a plan for you. Whose plan do you want to follow?

LESSON 12

SELF-CONTROL

*"to be **self-controlled**, pure, working at home, kind," (English Standard Version, Titus 2:5a).*

Older men are to be sober-minded, dignified, self-controlled. Did you see that in Titus 2:2?

Men are called to be self-controlled as women are. It's a fruit of the Spirit!

*"But the Holy Spirit produces this kind of fruit in our lives: love, joy, peace, patience,
kindness, goodness, faithfulness, [23] gentleness, and self-control. There is no law against
these things! [24] Those who belong to Christ Jesus have nailed the passions and desires of
their sinful nature to his cross and crucified them there. [25] Since we are living by the
Spirit, let us follow the Spirit's leading in every part of our lives. [26] Let us not become
conceited, or provoke one another, or be jealous of one another." (New Living*

Translation, Galatian 5:22-26)

YouTube: Francis Chan - Self Control https://www.youtube.com

or Francis Chan - The Toilet Bowl of Sin https://www.youtube.com

Ok, maybe you are asking, "What does this have to do with me? Self-controlled, pure, worker at home? I am not even married!"

Let me, as your leader, ask you this. Before you can get your driver permit, then license, what do you have to do?"

It amazes me that we prepared you when you were a teen, or still are a teen, more on how to drive a car and to learn the rules of the road, but we don't seem to do anything to prepare you for marriage and life. I have been married for over four decades, and it's hard and wonderful at the same time! There were times I wanted out! I bet my husband did also! But we knew we made a commitment before God. My husband and I both were born with a sin nature. We both have a tendency of pride and self-centeredness. We both had different personalities and had to learn to accept each other's differences and that one of us was not always right. We both had to learn self-control, or we might have killed each other! Ok, not literally.

Even as a teen, you have to learn self-control. I am sure there are times you are not happy with your parents' rules and may have let them know. You may have suffered the consequences of a lack of self-control of the tongue.

Look up the following verses on self-control.

II Peter 1:5-8

II Timothy 1:7

Proverbs 16:32

Titus 2:11-14

Galatians 5:19-23

Galatians 6:7-8

What happens when we ignore God and live only to satisfy ourselves (lack of self-control)?

What happens when we live to please the Spirit (self-control)?

Read James 3:1-18.

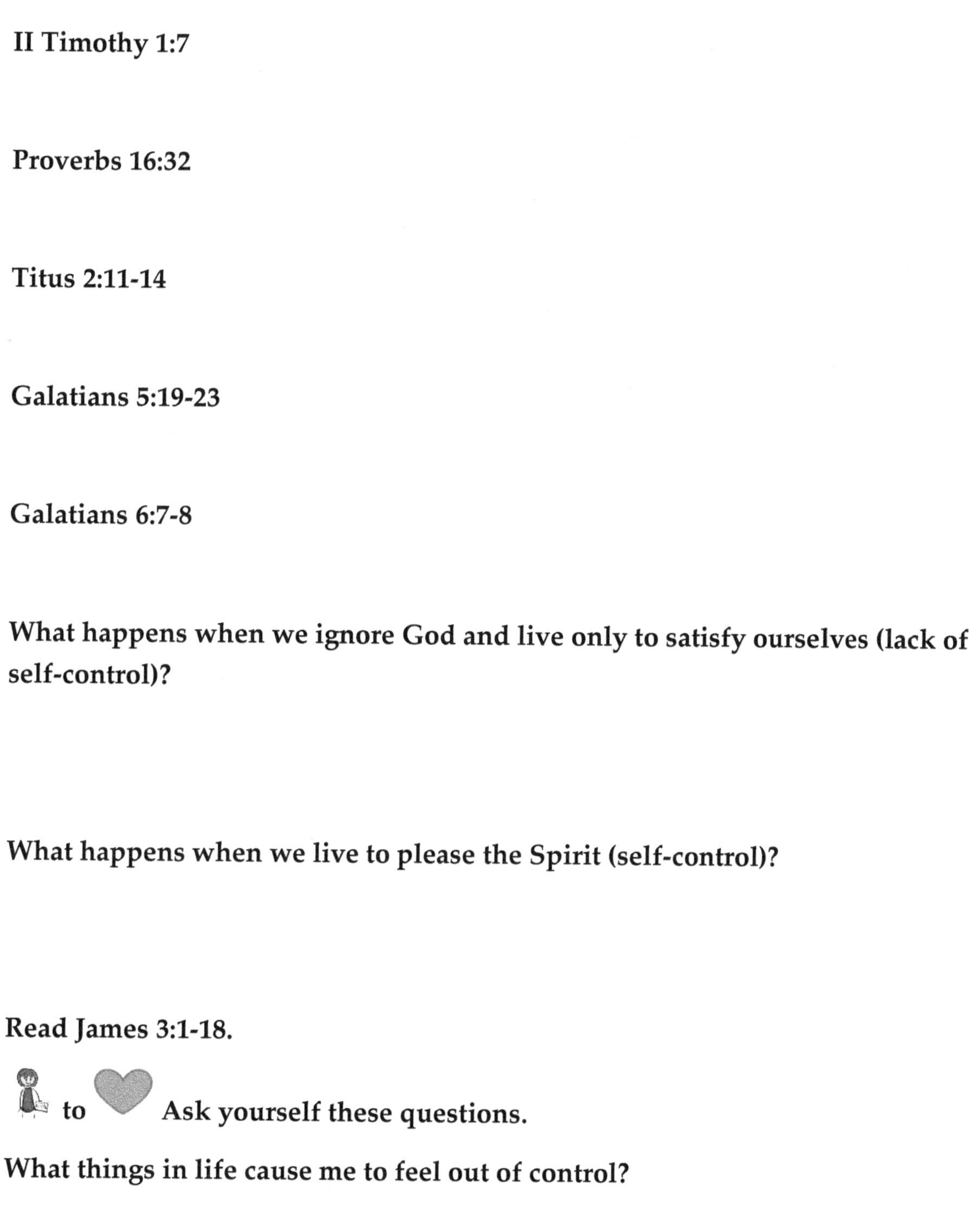

to Ask yourself these questions.

What things in life cause me to feel out of control?

How do I handle feeling out of control?

"Don't copy the behavior and customs of this world, but let God transform you into a new person by changing the way you think. Then you will learn to know God's will for you, which is good and pleasing and perfect." (NLT, Romans 12:2).

 **As a young adult, can I have self-control?**

How can I renew my mind?

Titus 2:5a says, "To be self-controlled, pure, working at home, kind,"

Now we hit the hard part of this verse. We are not going to go too deeply into this. It's interesting that we are first told to be self-controlled as the men are. Then we are told to be pure. Stuck in the middle of this verse is working at home." Then we are told to be kind. Odd order, or is it?

to Read I Timothy 5:13. What five things have these women learned to do?

Should they be doing these things?

Do girls do this?

Do you have to be married to be guilty of gossiping?

Why should we not be doing these things?

Read the last part of verse 5 in Titus 2. What are we doing to the Word of God?

Why do you think working at home is put in the middle? Could they be gossipers, going from home to home of friends, talking about each other? Just something to think about in regards to why it's there.

When we get older, and our children leave home, we realize how fast time went. It's time you never get back with your kids. Our kids are in our lives forever, hopefully! A job is not. A job will not come and visit you when you are old.

Finding the balance between work and kids is difficult. Something or someone suffers. We delude ourselves into thinking otherwise. There is only so much time in a day; eight to nine hours is taken up by a job, and kids maybe get four to five hours of their parents' time each day. Time is what they want, not things.

I am not putting down working parents. I worked when my kids were all in school. But my work consumed me. There was praise for a job well done. That never happens at home!   IF there is any way you can be home raising your children when they are babies to five years old, please do! No one can love them and teach them how to be the human beings you want them to be as much as you can. There is a security only you can build in them. So many opportunities to teach them about the Lord throughout your day can be missed. For me, when I came home from work, I was tired and it was hard to give my family time and energy.

There are moms who would love to stay home. Please know you are encourage to find the best balance for family and work.

"Should all mothers be stay-at-home moms?" Proverbs 31 is the well-known passage about the wife and mother of excellence. From the description of her, we learn that this mother did work outside of the home. However, her family never lacked anything. She maintained a proper balance, so her family never suffered. Her family was always her priority.

While the Bible leaves women the choice whether to stay at home with the children or go to work outside the home, it certainly is a commendable thing for a mother to be at home with the children and devote herself to training them full time. Women are encouraged in Titus 2 and I Timothy 5 to stay at home with their young children. Whatever a woman chooses, she must maintain her home as a priority and her primary sphere of influence.

LESSON 13

SUBMISSION

*"and **submissive** to their own husbands," (English Standard Version, Titus 2:5b)*

YouTube: Submission in Marriage https://www.youtube.com

"Then the LORD God said, 'It is not good for the man to be alone. I will make a helper who is just right for him.' 19 So the LORD God formed from the ground all the wild animals and all the birds of the sky. He brought them to the man[a] to see what he would call them, and the man chose a name for each one. 20 He gave names to all the livestock, all the birds of the sky, and all the wild animals. But still there was no helper just right for him" (New Living Translation, Genesis 2:18-20).

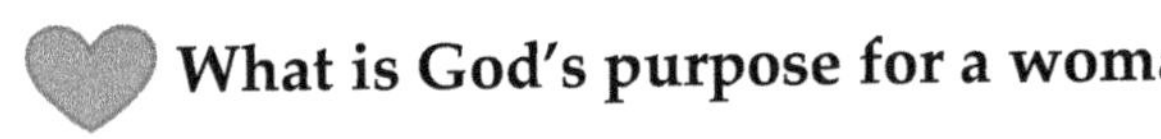

What is God's purpose for a woman?

In whose image is the woman created?

Are men and women equal in worth?

Do men and women have the same identical role in life? Back your answer with Scripture.

In Genesis 3:16, to the woman God said:

In Genesis 3:17, to Adam God said:

Even though we are equal in God's sight, women are more of the nurturer and care for the young, while men are better equipped to provide for and protect the family. Each has a different role to play in a Christian marriage. God created us this way. But we fight it, especially as women.

Genesis 3:16b *"your desire shall be for your husband, and he will rule over you."* Think about what this verse is saying. We, as women, want to be loved by our man. But, there is something else we want to do. We will desire to control our husbands. I know women who, shall we say, wear the pants in the family! I

have tried! The verse goes on to say, *"he will rule over you."* Does it sound like there would be a conflict in this house? It is the battle of the sexes!

As a young adult girl, have I noticed this in marriage relationships I have been around?

Does this verse mean a man is to rule over his wife? (Ephesians 5:25-30) We will get into this later.

If you answered "yes", use Scripture to back your answer.

When I was first married, I looked to my husband to fulfill my every need. (Just like the Bible said, *"your desire shall be for your husband".)*

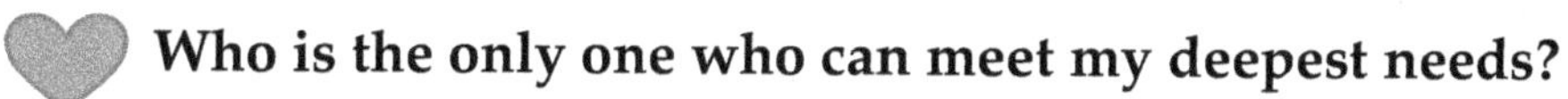

Who is the only one who can meet my deepest needs?

to **Do you see yourself looking to your boyfriend to meet your needs?**

Are we to have other gods?

When you are married, and you want your husband to meet all your needs, what kind of power do you give him? Could he use this to rule over you?

Now that you have looked deeper into Genesis 3:16b, do you see how this verse has been misquoted and misunderstood?

Ruling was a result of the fall. Man ruling over his wife was not God's original intent. Childbirth was not meant to be painful. The desire for substitute gods and all the pain in the world came because of the fall of man. If we think God's original plan was to have a man rule over his wife, then we have to include pain and brokenness as part of God's original intentions.

We are reminded in Titus 2 that older (mature) women are to teach the younger women to love their husbands and children. The older women had to learn. Because of the fall of man, it's not a natural desire in us. We have seen generation after generation of women who do not want to be submissive to their husbands. Many husbands, because of the fall, abused this submission because they are not under the submission of Christ.

Am I rebelling to the word 'submit'? I know I did until I learned what it meant. Let's take a trail and look it up.

SUBMIT = *Greek hupotasso. Better translated " to identify with" – "to be in support of" It has nothing to do with being subordinate to, secondary to, or subject to. The correct meaning is especially important and clear when considered against the cultural backdrop, that is to say, when it is understood in the light of the marriage customs and the culture of the people Paul was writing to.*
http://www.godswordtowomen.org/submit.htm

 **Who am I to submit to first? Write out James 4:7.**

Who else am I supposed to submit to according to Ephesians 5:21?

According to I Corinthians 11:2-3, what makes it easy for a wife to submit to her husband?

Who did Christ submit to in John 5:30?

Did Christ give up His worth? Do I give up my worth when I submit to my husband?

to **Some women have believed they needed to submit to every man. Read Ephesians 5:22-24. To whom is she only to submit?**

What is submission a picture of in verse 24?

What does I Peter 3:1 say about an unbelieving spouse?

When wives submit to their husbands, to whom are they submitting according to Ephesians 5:22?

To be fair, let's look at the husband's responsibility. Who does I Peter 3:7 say he will give an account to if he is selfish or domineering? He will give an account one day!

In Ephesians 5:25a, 28, 33a, what is a husband commanded to do?

What do we, as women, long for in marriage?

Girls, we are not off the hook! Read Ephesians 5:33b. Write it out.

Why are men commanded to love and why are women commanded to respect? (This changed my attitude as a wife when the Holy Spirit convicted me!)

Guys and girls are different! We have different needs in a dating relationship and marriage. A guy desires respect from his wife. A woman longs to be loved by her guy. A wife can deeply wound her husband when she disrespects him as a man. A woman who usurps authority (meaning taking control over every decision in the home) over her husband and takes away his leadership in the home is teaching her children unbiblical truths. We will be accountable to God. Also, girls, when you are married and tear down your husbands to others, we will answer to God for this disrespect. (Guys are not off the hook, but this study is not for them.)

Mark Gungor the Tale of Two Brains (You don't have to be married to enjoy this! The youth I showed it to saw how true this YouTube video was.)

https://www.bing.com/videos/search?q=mark+gungor+the+tale+of+two+brains

LESSON 14

HONOR GOD WITH OUR LIVES

"That the word of God may not be ***reviled****" (English Standard Version, Titus 2:5c)*

What does it mean "that the word of God may not be reviled"? Here are some other Bible translations of this verse. The Amplified version says, "so that the word of God may not be dishonored". The NIV says, "so that no one will malign the word of God". The New Living Translation says, "will not bring shame on the word of God". The Common English Bible says, "so that God's word won't be ridiculed". The Easy-to-Read says, "no one will be able to criticize the teaching God gave us".

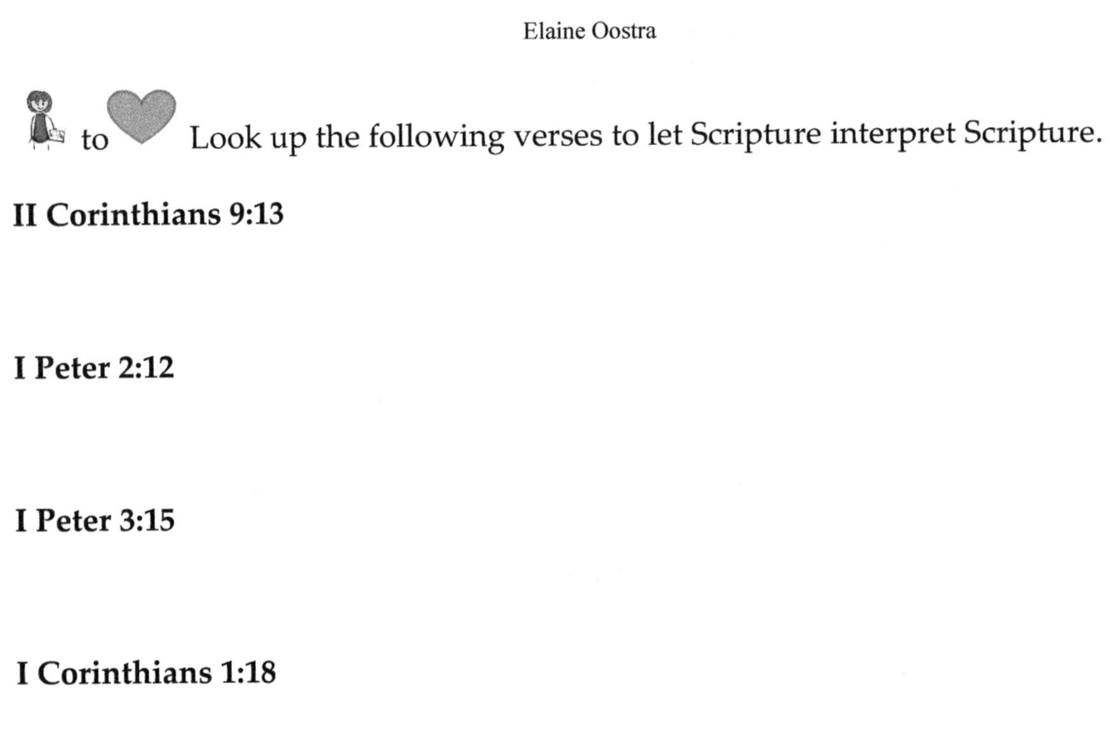

to Look up the following verses to let Scripture interpret Scripture.

II Corinthians 9:13

I Peter 2:12

I Peter 3:15

I Corinthians 1:18

Titus 2:7-10

Romans 8:7-8

Let's go a little deeper and understand God's calling on us as His people.

to **Why do you think God created you and me?**

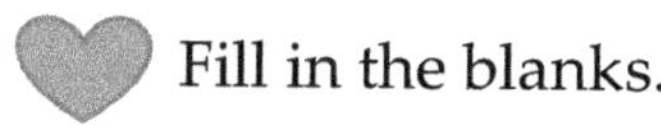

Fill in the blanks.

We are created for God's holiness NOT our happiness. Girls, if we focus on our happiness, we are in big trouble! Our emotions are too up and down daily!

In Colossians 1:16b, it says all things were created __________ and __________Him.

According to Ephesians 4:24, in whose likeness am I created?

According to Isaiah 43:7, in whose glory am I created and why?

Did you see anything in these verses about your personal happiness? Have you ever heard, "I divorced him because I wasn't happy and God wants me happy?" Excuse me, but which chapter and verse says it's about your happiness? Girls, DO NOT get married for personal happiness!

What is God's calling on my life as a believer as mentioned in I Peter 1:15-16?

This is a hard verse to comprehend. (The next lesson will explain how we can become holy.)

First, let's look at why some of you struggle with this passage in I Peter. When we have false standards of God's Word, we believe false teachings; we believe we are not required to live holy lives, and then we encourage others not to as well. Our enemy (Satan) creates a theology for believers to doubt. That leads to a perversion of God's Word. *Perversion means the alteration of something from its original course or meaning; a corruption of what was first intended.*

We live in a world that is perverting the True Gospel. None of us are smarter than God, yet we can act like we are.

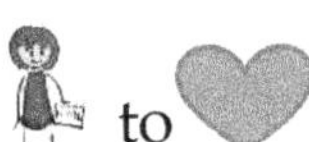 **Write out Hebrews 12:14.**

This is God's calling on my life and your life as a born again believer in Jesus Christ. If we do not get this understanding in our lives as believers in Jesus Christ, we dishonor God's Word. We believe the culture's way of thinking over God's unchanging Word. Jesus is the same yesterday, today, and tomorrow. We repress what we instinctively know in our conscience. We were born to know right from wrong, BUT we can come to a point where we no longer listen to our conscience. We legitimize wrong by legalizing it. God will let us have our way… for a time, giving us time to repent, because of His love for us!

LESSON 15

WHY GOD CREATED ME

Holiness in not an option for me as a Born-Again Believer in Jesus Christ.

We are all still in the process of learning what it means for us to be holy as God is Holy. God's Word is **Inerrantly Holy,** without any error. God is absent of even a trace of sin: His love is Holy, His mercy is Holy, His wrath is Holy, and His anger is Holy. Because of this, NO sin will be in Heaven to attack us! To be holy means to be set apart from the world. We need to live by God's standards and not the world's.

"For we are his workmanship, created in Christ Jesus for good works, which God prepared beforehand, that we should walk in them"(ESV, Ephesians 2:10).

SO HOW CAN WE BECOME HOLY?

We can't make ourselves holy, no matter how hard we try. So how can we become holy? Holiness only results from a right relationship with God by believing Jesus Christ as Savior.

Look up John 3:16 (yes, again).

Hebrews 12:2

We only increase in **practical holiness** (practicing, striving for, pursuing) as we mature spiritually. Pursuing holiness means we want to die to our sinful nature not encourage it or justify it. Before we were saved, we enjoyed our sin as we read in *Galatians 5:19-21 and I Corinthians 6:9-10.*

God has set us apart (being made holy) for honorable use.

Left on our own and even in a perfect world, being holy would never happen!

HOW GOD WORKS HOLINESS IN US

to **Write down something you are going through that is difficult in which you are questioning God.**

 **Read Romans 5:3-5. What are my suffering and trials producing in me?**

What has God given to me?

 **Read I Peter 1:6-7.**

 **What am I told to do in trials?**

Why is my faith tested?

What should be found?

 Bear with me; I have a point I am getting to!

 **Read Proverbs 17:3. What does the Lord do with my heart?**

How is God working holiness in me?

God is purifying us of sin; sin is unholy. Did you ever look at a trial in your life as God making you holy?

Read 11Corinthians 12:7-9, what is your 'thorn'(trial)? In verse 9 what is God wanting to teach you?

WHY DO WE WANT TO BECOME HOLY?

to According to II Timothy 2:12, what happens if we endure?

In reading James 1:2-4, what does testing of our faith produce? What is the perfect result?

to **On page 100 I had you write down a difficult situation you are going through. Now, write the following phrase above what you wrote with a different color pen:** "GOD IS IN THE PROCESS OF MAKING ME HOLY!"

This is my point! Yay! God uses our weakness (trials) so we can learn He our strength. We are complete, lacking in nothing! Girls, God is making us holy! Trials make us trust God more and trust less in our abilities, less of us and more of Him. God works this holiness in us. Because of our sinful nature, it usually takes trials to work holiness in us.

"Blessed is the man who remains steadfast under trial, for when he has stood the test he will receive the crown of life, which God has promised to those who love him" (ESV, James 1:12).

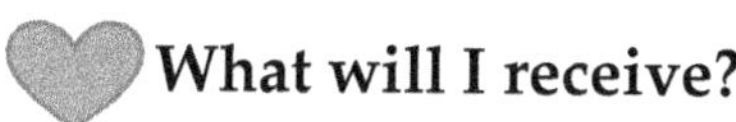
What will I receive?

This crown of life, girls, will be the most beautiful ornament we will ever wear! It will never wear out and it will never go out of style because it's eternal life with Jesus.

Well done, good and faithful girls! You endured a long study, but I pray your heart cries out for even more of God's Word. I pray there was an awakening in you by the power of the Holy Sprit to live as God has called you to. Will it be hard? Yes, but so full of peace and joy that cannot be stolen away because God put it there. Satan will try and take this away from you. Press even harder into God's Word, and you will become strong!

LEADERS GUIDE, LEADING A TEEN GIRL TO CHRIST

"If we confess our sins, He is faithful and just to forgive us" (ESV, I John 1:9).

Optional help on leading a teen girl into a relationship with Jesus Christ:

If you have not trusted in Jesus Christ, no matter how hard you try, the human nature is prone to sin. You can't get rid of it; only God can do it. We are all born with a desire to do what we want. That is a sin nature. We see it in babies on up. We demand our way. We cry when we don't get our way. We are selfish and self-centered; this is what sin is. It is us first on the throne of our lives. Like one of my daughters would say when she was two, "I do myself."

If you acknowledge that Jesus is Lord, recognizing His power and authority as God, and believe in your heart that God raised Him from the dead, you will be saved.

This is the good news that saves us, if we believe this message. Christ died for our sins, just as the Bible says. He was buried, and he was raised from the dead on the third day, just as the Bible says.

Here is a prayer for a new beginning:

Jesus, I do believe You are the Son of God and that You died on the cross to pay the penalty for my sin. Forgive me. I turn away from my sin and choose to live a life that pleases You. Enter my life as my Lord and Savior. I want to follow You and make You the leader of my life. Thank You for Your gift of eternal life and for the Holy Spirit, who has now come to live in me. I ask this in Your name, Amen

<u>**Question Worksheet Lesson 1**</u>

INSECURE VS SECURE

How can I relate to Stephanie?

If someone compliments me, what do I reply back? (Share what you would say).

(If you are comfortable in your group, share) Which one of the girls am I: 1.Confident, 2. Conceited or 3. Insecure?

Share what I think it means to *draw attention to myself.* Could it be the opposite of decent and appropriate?

Share what I Timothy 2:10 says should draw others to me.

Share how I can make myself attractive by the things I do or how I present myself.

What, as a teen girl, draws me to an older woman as a mentor? Is it her body shape, hair, how she dresses? What is it?

How do I want someone to be drawn to me?

Question Worksheet Lesson 2

HOW CAN I OVERCOME INSECURITY?

I am a daughter of the living God! (Share who God said you are.)

When I am feeling insecure, how can I know what it looks like to attain true security?

Does this insecurity describe me?

Do I have this confidence in Christ where I trust him fully with my life?

In Jude 24, who can keep me from stumbling?

According to John 3:16, what do I have as a believer in Christ?

In Ephesians 2:8-9, who saved me?

According to John 14:6, who is the truth and the way and the life for me?

Where does I Timothy 6:17 tell me to put my hope?

According to Jeremiah 17:7-8, what does it look like when I trust God?

According to Psalm 9:10, will God forsake me when I trust in Him?

According to Deuteronomy 31:8, does God ever leave me?

In Lamentations 3:57, what does God say to me?

Read Matthew 6:31-34, does God know what I need?

According to Philippians 4:19, what will God supply for me?

According to Isaiah 26:3, where do I need to put my mind?

When I struggle with feelings of insecurity, (and yes, we still will at times) who do I need to trust?

What happens when I stay in my insecurity and miss the peace of God?

How does this affect the ability to know who I am in Christ?

Who wants to keep me insecure? Read I Peter 5:8 and Ephesians 6:10-18.

So, what can I do? (James 4:7)

Is there a difference between being self-confident and being confident because of who I am in Christ?

How does knowing my identity in Christ makes me confident?

<u>Question Worksheet Lesson 3</u>

MY IDENTITY IN CHRIST CAN MAKE ME CONFIDENT?

How did I see Candace change the way she saw herself after finding her identity in Christ?

Did she ever say that her confidence came from self?

Where did Candace get her confidence?

What can I learn from Candace?

In what ways do I put confidence in my flesh?

What does a fool do? *"The wise are cautious and avoid danger; fools plunge ahead with reckless confidence" (NLT, Proverbs 14:16).*

According to Galatians 5:17, what are the desires of the flesh and what are the desires of the Spirit?

What does 'self' usually tell me to do?

My sinful nature wants me to ________ which is the opposite of what the __________ wants.

What happens when I follow the desires of my sinful nature? (Galatians 5:19-21)

II Corinthians 3:4-5, *"Such is the confidence and steadfast reliance and absolute trust that we have through Christ toward God.* [5] *Not that we are sufficiently qualified in ourselves to claim anything as coming from us,* ***but*** *our sufficiency and qualifications come from God."* **In trusting Christ, what can I have according to verse 4?**

Where does this sufficiency and qualification come from according to verse 5b? Did it say anything about 'self '?

What do I see as the difference between my self-confidence and confidence through Christ? Is it different than what I thought?

Confidence. In the following verses, (circle) where your confidence (*trust)* comes from and (underline) what you are to do with your confidence.

Ephesians 3:11-12, "*This was his eternal plan, which he carried out through Jesus Christ our Lord. Because of Christ and our faith in him, we can now come boldly and confidently into God's presence."*

Hebrews 3:6, *"But Christ, as the Son, is in charge of God's entire house. And we are God's house, if we keep our courage and remain confident in our hope in Christ."*

Hebrews 3:14, *"For if we are faithful to the end, trusting God just as firmly as when we first believed, we will share in all that belongs to Christ."*

Hebrews 4:16, *"Let us then with confidence draw near to the throne of grace, that we may receive mercy and find grace to help in time of need."*

I John 4:16-17, "*We know how much God loves us, and we have put our trust in his love. God is love, and all who live in love live in God and God lives in them. And as we live in God, our love grows more perfect. So we will not be afraid on the day of judgment."*

I John 5:14, *"And we are confident that he hears us whenever we ask for anything that pleases him."*

Hebrews 10:32b, 35, "*...remember how you remained faithful even though it meant terrible suffering." "So do not throw away this confident trust in the Lord. Remember the great reward it brings you!"*

Hebrews 10:17 and 19, *"Then he says, 'I will never again remember their sins and lawless deeds.'" "And so, dear brothers and sisters, we can boldly enter heaven's Most Holy Place because of the blood of Jesus."*

Share how my confidence in Christ makes me more hopeful in struggles I may be facing at school, home, and maybe family? How am I encouraged in my personal relationship with Christ?

Question Worksheet Lesson 4

KNOWING TRUTH – SOUND DOCTRINE

What does it mean that God is my Father?

What am I worshipping?

How do I live out what the Bible says?

What is the most important thing in my life?

Who determines what is right or wrong?

If it doesn't hurt anyone, then why does it matter?

How does God save people?

What does Mark 9:42 say about the importance of my leaders not teaching me false doctrine? "*But if you cause one of these little ones who trusts in me to fall into sin, it would be better for you to have a large millstone tied around your neck and be drowned in the depths of the sea.*"

I need to think about this; if I don't have correct biblical doctrine, how can I get God's truth for my life?

Where does God's Word come from?

What is it for?

How can it change me?

Underline where God's Word comes from and circle what it's for and how it can change me.

II Timothy 3:16, "*All Scripture is inspired by God and is useful to teach us what is true and to make us realize what is wrong in our lives. It corrects us when we are wrong and teaches us to do what is right.*"
II Peter 1:20-21, "*for no prophecy recorded in Scripture was ever thought up by the*

prophet himself. It was the Holy Spirit within these godly men who gave them true messages from God."

Read what these verses say that true doctrine (teaching) is and what false doctrine (teaching) is that I need to know. Underline true teaching and circle false teaching.

II Timothy 4:2-4, *"Preach the word of God. Be prepared, whether the time is favorable or not. Patiently correct, rebuke, and encourage your people with good teaching. For a time is coming when people will no longer listen to sound and wholesome teaching. They will follow their own desires and will look for teachers who will tell them whatever their itching ears want to hear. They will reject the truth and chase after myths."*

II Tim 1:13, *"Hold on to the pattern of wholesome teaching you learned from me—a pattern shaped by the faith and love that you have in Christ Jesus."*

II Timothy 3:5, *"They will act religious, but they will reject the power that could make them godly. Stay away from people like that!"*

I Timothy 1:3-4, *"When I left for Macedonia, I urged you to stay there in Ephesus and stop those whose teaching is contrary to the truth. Don't let them waste their time in endless discussion of myths and spiritual pedigrees. These things only lead to meaningless speculations, which don't help people live a life of faith in God."*

I Timothy 6:3-5, *"Some people may contradict our teaching, but these are the wholesome teachings of the Lord Jesus Christ. These teachings promote a godly life. Anyone who teaches something different is arrogant and lacks understanding. Such a person has an unhealthy desire to quibble over the meaning of words. This stirs up arguments ending in jealousy, division, slander, and evil suspicions. These people always* *cause trouble. Their minds are corrupt, and they have turned their backs on the truth. To them, a show of godliness is just a way to become wealthy."*

II Peter 1:20-21, *"Above all, you must realize that no prophecy in Scripture ever came from the prophet's own understanding or from human initiative. No, those prophets were moved by the Holy Spirit, and they spoke from God."*

I John 4:1, *"Dear friends, do not believe everyone who claims to speak by the Spirit. You must test them to see if the spirit they have comes from God. For there are many false prophets in the world."*

What is the warning to teachers regarding what they present to me as truth?
I Timothy 4:16, "*Keep a close watch on how you live and on your teaching. Stay true to what is right for the sake of your own salvation and the salvation of those who hear you."*

How easily can I be lead astray if my leader doesn't know or understand the authority in which God speaks?

Do I have a better understanding of the importance of sound doctrine?

Question Worksheet Lesson 5

GODLY LIVING

Do I want the woman with the erratic behavior as a mentor in my life or the woman Leslie talks about with reverent behavior and a desire for God.

Do I think reverent behavior is just for the "older woman"?

*"I **want you** to know how much I have agonized for **you** and for the church at Laodicea, and for many other believers who have never met me personally. [2] I **want** them to be encouraged and knit together by strong ties of love. I **want** them to have complete confidence that they understand God's mysterious plan, which is Christ himself. [3] In him lie hidden all the treasures of **wisdom** and **knowledge**." (NLT, Colossians 2:1-3).*

What does verse 1 and 2 want for me?

What two treasures are not hidden from me, but for me, in Christ in verse 3?

Underline what I am instructed to do when I am in Christ.

"Therefore, as you received Christ Jesus the Lord, so walk in him, rooted and built up in him and established in the faith, just as you were taught, abounding in thanksgiving" (ESV, Colossians 2: 6-7).

"And you, who were dead in your trespasses and the uncircumcision of your flesh, God made alive together with him, having forgiven us ALL our trespasses" (ESV, Colossians 2:13). **What did Christ Jesus do for me?**

" But God is so rich in mercy, and he loved us so much, [5] that ***even though we were dead because of our sins****, he gave us life when he raised Christ from the dead. (It is only by God's grace that you have been saved!) [6] For he raised us from the dead along with Christ and* ***seated us with him in the heavenly realms*** *because we are united with* ***Christ Jesus"*** *(NLT, Ephesians 2:4 -6).*

When did God love me?

With whom am I seated and where?

Who saved me?

"For by grace you have been (perfect tense) saved through faith. And this Is ***not your own doing****; it is the* ***gift of God*** *not a result of works, so that no one may boast" (ESV, Ephesians 2:8).* **Why can't I save myself?**

Write out John 10:28. Who gave me eternal life?

Who has me in His hand?

How secure am I in His hand?

According to I Peter 1:5, what will God do for me in His mighty power?

Do I truly take all this to heart?

Why do I turn to other 'things' to find my worth?

Do I think what Christ did for me is not enough?

When I don't find my worth in what Christ did for me, I can't give it to the next generation. True or False?

Can you see that when you know your worth in Christ, this spurs you to want to live for Him, to live to glorify Him, and not glorify ourselves (in gossiping, which tears others down). If we don't understand who we are in Christ, we won't have the urge to live godly, reverent lives. **Do you agree or disagree? Why or why not? Share with the group.**

If we don't have reverence for God, we will not have reverence for others. We will put others down, become slanderers, making others seem lesser than us. If we indulge (don't be slaves to much wine) in what makes us happy, life becomes all about "me." Self-centeredness is what makes girls-women feel free to put others down.

Share as a group maybe how this has been done to you, or maybe you have done this to a girl at school. Ask God to help you forgive someone who has put you down, or ask God to help you to apologize to someone you may have put down. Repentance and forgiveness set us free and help us to grow in confidence!

Question Worksheet Lesson 6

RENOUNCING UNGODLINESS

Share in your group what I see is ungodliness and worldly passion?

Why do I have to be trained to renounce it?

When I read the prayer in Daniel 9:3-15, I need to think about why a godly man like Daniel would include himself with the sins of the people.

What did Daniel acknowledge? Did I notice that he included himself in what they had been doing wrong? (To me he was a pretty righteous guy!)

When praying for our nation, have I ever thought of confessing myself as part of the sin in our nation? Can I say, "We have sinned"?

In Daniel 9:16-19, what is Daniel's plea?

Did Daniel come before God in his own righteousness? If not, then how?

In Romans 3:10, who is righteous?

According to Romans 3:23-25, who sinned?

What did God do?

How am I made right with God?

Question Worksheet Lesson 7

MEANING OF LOVE – STORGE AND EROS

Before we start, I want you to write down or talk about what you think the word 'love' means. When we are done with the lesson on love, I want you to look at what you wrote down and see if it's the same as what you are about to learn.

STORGE

What does this love, storge, look like in Romans 12:9-10?

Can you think of some examples of storge love?

When this kind of love is perverted or lost, what happens to humans in Romans 1:28-32 and II Timothy 3:3?

Why would someone be without love?

Who or what do I think has a hold of this person's heart? (Mark 7:21)

EROS

This type of love needs proper boundaries. What are they in I Corinthians 7:8-9?

Hebrews 13:4

I Corinthians 7:5

"Eros love is part of God's design, a gift of his goodness for procreation and enjoyment. Sex, as God intended it, is a source of delight and a beautiful blessing between a man and a woman who are married to each other." (Sam O'Neal)

How does Proverbs 5:18-19 support this?

What do I see in the world that has happened when eros is outside of God's plan?

God's plan for marriage is not built on eros love. ***It's conditional and depends on being attracted to the other person. It causes affairs in marriage. It's a very self-centered love.***

Is this the kind of love I want, love that only gives to receive?

If I give myself sexually to a guy who says he loves me and then the next day, or so I see him with someone else, what do I think will happen to my heart?

A guy gives love to get sex; a girl gives sex to get love. True or False?

Why do I think marriage will not last if it's built on eros love?

Do I want the guy I am going to marry to love me unconditionally?

With eros love, what happens when a guy no longer finds me attractive?

What security do I have in a relationship if I move in with my boyfriend? Are we honestly committed to each other?

What does Romans 1:27 tell me about what happens when I believe we can go outside the boundaries of God's Word and then encourage others to do the same?

Why, as a Christian, would I want others to receive a due penalty? Roman 1: 32 tells us it's the death penalty. Doesn't this make my heart sad?

Read Romans 1:24-32 in full context. How am I sending others to their death by justifying their sin?

Are there any Scriptures that support a sexual relationship that is not just between a married man and woman? Does this matter?

Is man wiser than God in how He created our bodies to function?

How do I define what sin is if I don't believe what God says?

If I decide myself what I can do sexually and I have no moral law, what could happen? Could little children be sexually abused?

Read Leviticus 18:6-23 and see what would be acceptable if I don't believe God's Word. (Where the verse says "do not", replace with "I think they can because I love them and accept them as they are.")

According to II Corinthians 11:2-4, how can my pure devotion to Christ be led astray when I listen to a false teaching that is not in God's Word?

<u>Question Worksheet Lesson 8</u>

MY HEART

"The seed of every sin is in every heart." (quote by John Owen)

According to Matthew 7:2-5, who has the speck and who has the log?

What am I to do first?

After I do my part, then what can I do?

In Romans 3:23, what do I read that we all have done and fallen short of?

These next verses may be hard to look at in I Corinthians and Galatians. <u>Underline</u> <u>each sin</u> we are capable of because we are born with a sin nature. Yes, we are born that way. We each struggle with the different tendency of sin. I sure had my struggles with sins listed below! But without truth, there is no conviction.

9"Don't you realize that those who do wrong will not inherit the Kingdom of God?
Don't fool yourselves. Those who indulge in sexual sin, or who worship idols, or commit
adultery, or are male prostitutes, or practice homosexuality, 10 or are thieves, or greedy
people, or drunkards, or are abusive, or cheat people—none of these will inherit the
Kingdom of God.11 Some of you were once like that. But you were cleansed; you were
made holy; you were made right with God by calling on the name of the Lord Jesus Christ
and by the Spirit of our God" (NLT, I Corinthians 6:9-11).

"When you follow the desires of your sinful nature, the results are very clear: sexual immorality, impurity, lustful pleasure, idolatry, sorcery, hostility, quarreling, jealousy, outbursts of anger, selfish ambition, dissension, division, envy, drunkenness, wild parties, and other sins like these. Let me tell you again, as I have before, that anyone living that sort of life will not inherit the Kingdom of God"(NLT, Galatians 5:19-21).

What have those who belong to Christ Jesus done? (Galatians 5:24) (This is what I do with my struggles with sin!)

According to I Corinthians 6:9-10, what was I before I believed? Do I see that none of us are without sin?

How is verse 11 full of hope in I Corinthians 6?

What happens to my old life in II Corinthians 5:17?

When I justify someone's sin because I think I am loving them, what does I Corinthians 6:11 tell me I am withholding from them?

Verse 10b of I Corinthians 6 says, *"none of these will inherit the Kingdom of God"*. **Who are the none? Do I believe what God is saying? Or do I believe my culture?**

How is it loving to withhold the truth of God's Word from those who are perishing?

What does God desire when I and others sin? (II Peter 3:9)

How does John 3:16 make this possible?

In John 3:20, what keeps me and others from eternal life?

Use these verses to answer the following questions:

"Run from sexual sin! No other sin so clearly affects the body as this one does. For sexual immorality is a sin against your own body. [19] Don't you realize that your body is the temple of the Holy Spirit, who lives in you and was given to you by God? You do not belong to yourself, [20] for God bought you with a high price. So you must honor God with your body" (NLT, I Corinthians 6:18-20).

(Verse 18b) Sexual immorality is a sin __________your own__________ .

(Verse 19) My body is the ______ of the _____ ________ .

Who lives in me?

Who gave me my body?

Do I have the right to do with my body whatever I want? (Verse 19)

Who do I belong to, who bought me, and who lives in me?

After reading these verses, how does a sexual sin against my body hurt my body more than any other sin? (I will reword it this way, how can sexual immorality consume your flesh and your body and your heart and your mind more destructively than any other sin?)

According to I Peter 1:15-16, how am I to live?

In Roman 12:1-2, what is my body to be?

<u>**Question Worksheet Lesson 9**</u>

MEANING OF LOVE - PHILEO AND AGAPE

I Thessalonians 4:9

I Samuel 18:1-3

Romans 12:10

Hebrews 13:1

In Jude 1:1b, what name does Jude have for those who are called?

AGAPE is our final love and most important one.

Read **Matthew 5:44**

In John 3:16, what did God do for me while I was still unresponsive, unkind, unlovable, and unworthy?

Agape love is beautifully described in I Corinthians 13. Write down what love:

IS -

IS NOT –

What is agape love? Write out the following Scriptures.

John 17:26

Romans 5:5, 8

Galatians 5:22

In John 13:35 and I John 3:16, what does this love look like for me?

Girls, summarize what you learned about the word 'love'.

What kind of love should I have toward my spouse one day? Toward my children ? Family? Friends?

How has the study of the word 'love' helped me understand God's love for me more?

Do I see how God's love is unconditional and our love is conditional?

Question Worksheet Lesson 10

PATTERN FOR MARRIAGE

Read Genesis 2:18-25. What is the first thing God said about the man?

What was fashioned from the rib? (Genesis 2:22)

Go back to Genesis 2:7. How did God make Adam?

What did God breathe into Adam? (This breath is spiritual, mental, and physical into the one to bear His image!)

Read and write out Job 33:4.

How did God create animals, fish, and birds? (Genesis 2:19)

What did God use to create man and woman? (He used dust and breath and His hands. Did you see this?)

Physical Breath

Is God still forming us today and breathing life into us? (Psalm 139:13-14)

Spiritual Breath *"Humans can reproduce only human life, but the Holy Spirit gives birth to spiritual life.*[a] *7 So don't be surprised when I say, 'You*[b] *must be born again.' 8 The wind blows wherever it wants. Just as you can hear the wind but can't tell where it comes from or where it is going, so you can't explain how people are born of the Spirit" (NLT, John 3:6-8).*

How is spiritual breath different than physical breath?

In Genesis 2:23, Adam is awake. What does he say?

In Genesis 2:24, how is the standard of all future marriages defined?

In Matthew 19:4-6, how did God make Adam and Eve? What shall the two become? What are they not?

In Romans 8:7, why is the world changing what God has ordained for marriage?

<u>Question Worksheet Lesson 11</u>

MARRIAGE AS A COVENANT. WHAT?

What is a covenant? Have you ever heard of the word covenant referring to marriage?

The first mention of marriage being a covenant is found in Malachi 2:14, 15, *"Because the Lord was witness between you and the wife of your youth, to whom you have been faithless, though she is your companion and your wife by* ***covenant.*** *Did he not make them one, with a portion of the Spirit in their union? And what was the one God seeking?* ***Godly offspring.*** *So guard yourselves in your spirit, and let none of you be faithless to the wife of your youth."*

What does this passage teach about marriage and children?

What did Christ shed for me on the cross? Why? (I John 1:7 and Romans 5:9)

When God created our bodies, He placed in women **a hymen**.

Did you ever wonder why?

Look up Ephesians 5:31, what do man and woman become when they leave their father and their mother?

There are many reasons God ordained marriage. Let's look up some verses.

Genesis 2:18

Malachi 2:13-16

What is God seeking? (Verse 15)

Why does God want me to be faithful to my spouse? (Verse 16)

What am I protected from in marriage? (I Corinthians 7:2)

What does Proverbs 18:22 say about marriage? (If you have a Message version, look it up in there and other versions.)

Read Ephesians 5:25-26 and answer the following questions:

What did Christ do for His bride?

How is this an example of what husbands are to do?

For wives, when you become one, you are not off the hook. What are we to do according to Ephesians 5:22-24?

When will the bride of Christ, the Church (us) be united with Him? (Revelation 19:7-9, 21:1-2 and 22:20)

Can I remain unmarried? (I Corinthians 7:7-9, 32-35,37)

When should I be married? (I Corinthians 7:1-2)

Do you now have a better understanding of the covenant of marriage? Share what you have learned. How is it different than when I first asked you what a covenant was?

Why is it important for me to understand why God ordained marriage?

Question Worksheet Lesson 12

SELF-CONTROL

Before I can get my driver permit, then license, what do I have to do?

Look up the following verses on self-control.

II Peter 1:5-8

II Timothy 1:7

Proverbs 16:32

Titus 2:11-14

Galatians 5:19-23

Galatians 6:7-8

What happens when I ignore God and live only to satisfy myself (lack of self-control)?

What happens when I live to please the Spirit (self-control)?

James 3:1-18

Ask yourself these questions:

What things in life cause me to feel out of control?

How do I handle feeling out of control?

"Don't copy the behavior and customs of this world, but let God transform you into a new person by changing the way you think. Then you will learn to know God's will for you, which is good and pleasing and perfect" (NLT, Romans 12:2).

As a young adult, can I have self-control?

How can I renew my mind?

Titus 2:5a, "To be self-controlled, pure, working at home, kind". Odd order, or is it?

Read I Timothy 5:13. What five things have these women learned to do?

Should they be doing these things?

Do girls do this?

Do I have to be married to be guilty of gossiping?

Why should I not be doing these things?

Read last part of verse 5 in Titus 2. What are we doing to the Word of God?

Why do you think working at home is put in the middle? Could they be gossipers, going from home to home to their friends talking about each other? Just something to think about.

Question Worksheet Lesson 13

SUBMISSION

"Then the LORD God said, "It is not good for the man to be alone. I will make a helper who is just right for him." [19] So the LORD God formed from the ground all the wild animals and all the birds of the sky. He brought them to the man[a] to see what he would call them, and the man chose a name for each one. [20] He gave names to all the livestock, all the birds of the sky, and all the wild animals. But still there was no helper just right for him." (NLT, Genesis 2:18-20).

What is God's purpose for a woman?

In whose image is the woman created?

Are men and women equal in worth?

Do men and women have the same identical role in life? Back your answer with Scripture.

In Genesis 3:16, to the woman God said:

In Genesis 3:17, to Adam God said:

Genesis 3:16b says, *"Your desire shall be for your husband, and he will rule over you."* Think about what this verse is saying. We, as women, want to be loved by our man. But, there is something else we want to do. We will desire to control our husbands. I know women who, shall we say, wear the pants in the family! I have tried! The verse goes on to say, *"he will rule over you."* Does this sound like there would be a conflict in this house! It is the battle of the sexes!

As a teen, have I noticed this in marriage relationships I have been around?

Does this verse mean a man is to rule over his wife? (Ephesians 5:25-30)

If you answered "yes", use Scripture to back your answer.

Who only can meet my deepest needs?

Do I see myself looking to my boyfriend to meet my needs?

Am I to have other gods?

When I am married, and I want my husband to meet all my needs, what kind of power do I give him? Could he use this to rule over me?

Now that I have looked deeper into Genesis 3:16b, do I see how this verse has been misquoted and misunderstood?

Am I rebelling to the word 'submit'?

Who am I to submit to first? Write out James 4:7.

Who else am I supposed to submit to according to Ephesians 5:21?

According to I Corinthians 11:2-3, what makes it easy for a wife to submit to her husband?

Who did Christ submit to in John 5:30?

Did Christ give up his worth?

Do I have to give up my worth when I submit to my husband?

Some women have believed they needed to submit to every man. Read Ephesians 5:22-24. To whom is she only to submit?

What is submission a picture of in verse 24?

What does I Peter 3:1 say about an unbelieving spouse?

When wives submit to their husbands, to whom are they submitting according to Ephesians 5:22?

To be fair, let's look at the husband's responsibility. Who does I Peter 3:7 say he will give an account to if he is selfish or domineering? He will give an account one day!

In Ephesians 5:25a, 28, 33a, what is a husband commanded to do?

What do we, as women, long for in marriage?

Girls, we are not off the hook! Read Ephesians 5:33b. Write it out.

Why are men commanded to love and why are women commanded to respect? (This changed my attitude as a wife when the Holy Spirit convicted me!)

Question Worksheet Lesson 14

HONOR GOD WITH OUR LIVES

What does it mean "that the word of God may not be reviled?" Look up the following verses to let Scripture interpret Scripture.

II Corinthians 9:13

I Peter 2:12

I Peter 3:15

I Corinthians 1:18

Titus 2:7-10

Romans 8:7-8

Why do you think God created you and me?

We are created for God's holiness NOT our happiness. Girls, if we focus on our happiness, we are in big trouble! Our emotions are too up and down daily!

Colossians 1:16b says that all things were created __________ and __________Him.

According to Ephesians 4:24, in whose likeness am I created?

Read Isaiah 43:7. In whose glory am I created and why?

What is God's calling on my life as a believer as mentioned in I Peter 1:15-16?

Write out Hebrews 12:14

Question Worksheet Lesson 15

WHY GOD CREATED ME

HOW CAN WE BECOME HOLY?

Look up John 3:16 (yes, again) .

Hebrews 12:2

HOW GOD WORKS HOLINESS IN US

I want you to write down something you are going through that is difficult in which you are questioning God.

Read Romans 5:3-5. What is my suffering and trials producing in me?

What has God given to me?

Read I Peter 1:6-7. What am I told to do in trials?

Why is my faith tested?

What should be found?

Read Proverbs 17:3. What does the Lord do with my heart?

How is God working holiness in me?

God is purifying me of sin; sin is unholy. Did I ever look at a trial in my life as God making me holy?

I had you write down a difficult situation you are going through. Now, I want you to write the following phrase above what you wrote with a different color of pen, "GOD IS IN THE PROCESS OF MAKING ME HOLY!"

11Corinthians12:7-9

WHY DO WE WANT TO BECOME HOLY?
According to II Timothy 2:12, what happens if I endure?

In reading James 1:2-4, what does the testing of my faith produce?

What is the perfect result?

***"Blessed is the man who remains steadfast under trial, for when he has stood the test he will receive the crown of life, which God has promised to those who love him"* (ESV, James 1:12).**

What will I receive?

ROLE MODELS

What a better way to end this study than to read testimonies of girls and women who had another woman in their life who has made an impact on them. I had fun collecting these letters. Notice when you read how ordinary women that are mentioned by the writer have made an impact. I hope this encourages you! Teaching the younger women can be done in a Bible study, but mainly it's our lifestyle that needs to reflect Christ. In reading these letters, you will also read what the younger women see in us as the mature women. They are watching us!

Anna E. (Age 20)

Throughout middle school, I didn't really have women in my life that I could go to for help. In high school, that all changed. Everywhere I looked I had role models that I could go to. For example, I had my high school counselor, librarian, and my grandma. Now that I am in college I find myself still using these ladies as role models. I also have made new friends and have found that I can trust one friend in particular.

My high school counselor and librarian have helped me deal with friendship and depression. High school people are not nice to others and being someone who doesn't feel like they fit in just made it that much harder to socialize with others around me. They would give me tips on how to approach people and ask if I could hang out. Being born with a disability, it was hard for me to do school work, let alone hang out with friends. I can still do the same stuff my friends were doing, but I couldn't do everything.

My grandma has helped me learn to love me for who I am. She also taught me how to think differently about life. I tend to focus on the negatives. My grandma would remind me about the simple things in life and use those as positive things in life. My grandma has also shown me what it means to live by faith, not just read it.

I see my grandma read her Bible and pray and she has a very positive outlook on life (as far as I can see). She always makes time and room for God and her Bible. I am off and on in this aspect. I know that it's an excuse to say "Oh I'm too busy" or "I don't have time", but as my high school counselor said: "If God laid down His life and took the time for that, then you have time to pray and give Him time."

The last quote from high school that has stuck with me is from my librarian. "Prayer doesn't have to be long and thoughtful. It can be short and sweet and still have the same meaning." What I got from that is I don't have to make it a long prayer. It can just be a short little prayer about anything like a test in school or a family issue that is going on.

Sydney Sue (Age 15)

I have always loved Betsey. I have pictures of her holding me as a toddler, and I find that extraordinary that I am still connected to her today. Every time I see her, I can't help but smile. She just has that way about her. I remember the first time I realized how much she loved God.

A few years ago (2013), she got up at our youth church camp and sang an original song. Being only 13 at the time, I wasn't emotional, but the way she closed her eyes and poured her heart and soul into that song made me cry. Flash forward to last year's (2015) church camp where we had altar night. Again, even at 15, I still never was an emotional crier, but that night I started to tear up as everyone around me was crying. Finally, I let the tears shed, and I poured out myself to God, and I gave Him everything: my family, my possessions, my problems, everything.

I made eye contact with Betsey, and I sat by her and told her everything. After patiently listening, she finally said, "You're free, Sydney." She then prayed over me and what was shocking was that I didn't think that it was Betsey that was talking to me, but God. God talked to me that night through Betsey. Through her, it was the first time I felt like I got answers from Him. When we worshiped later that night, she threw her hands up in the air and praised and praised and praised. She showed me that it's okay to give yourself over to Him. It's okay to throw your hands up in the air and praise. It's okay to be yourself.

Betsey has given me so much. She makes me feel loved and wanted. She makes me feel like I'm worth something when I feel low. I can always count on her to listen to all my problems. She made me realize that we are all human and we are all pretty screwed up somehow. Even Betsey has a dark past that brought me to tears, but in that darkness is when we shine the brightest.

She has not only done so much for me, but also for my church. She works there, but I never feel like it's a job for her. She wants to be there. You can always count on Betsey to give you a hug or kiss. That's just who she is. However, my favorite thing about Betsey is that even though it isn't my middle name, she is the only one to call me Sydney Sue. She truly is a blessing. I love you, Betsey!

Joanna C (Age 28)

Wow, I wish I could summarize in one paragraph or two an answer to mentors in my life, but I can't! There have been so many amazing women who have poured into my life, praying over me, speaking into my challenges, and setting honest examples for me.

I think of my youth leader in middle school and high school who shared with me the struggles she had when growing up and who was open with me about challenges in her married life and who took me one-on-one to a number of different places just to hang out. She is someone who patterned for me what it means to go up to a young girl at church and take them out to do something.

I think of the women who I ran to when tired and emotionally exhausted who refueled my fire for Jesus by praying over me, hugging me, studying the Word with me, etc. (yes, you're included, Elaine), either over the phone or in person. I think of one woman who did a cooking class and a Bible study with me and a couple of others as a middle school student. I've cooked ever since.

I could tell you story after story of Barb, Elaine, Helen, Karen, Diane, Annette, Sigrid, etc., etc., and the list goes on and on. Their stories of their failings are so real, and yet I feel warmth when they open their lives to me and tell me how wonderful I am and how proud of me they are or simply when they just really listen and offer support by being an emotional cushion. This is what being a Christian is all about to me. It's about this deep need that only Christ's love and the love we have for each other can fill. I know I wouldn't be the missionary I am today without them. Where would I be without so many wonderful women of God who have backed me all these years? And don't even get me started on my mom!

Sue G (Age 61)

In my Coffee Break Bible Study, it was wonderful in my 40s to have a lesson each week with a woman who is now 102. Her sharing as a Bible study leader was a gentle blessing. How wonderful to have the Scriptures. The Holy Spirit would apply that individually to my heart to inspire and build me up. She was there, but I didn't have to get too personal if I didn't want to.

While being in an Al-Anon recovery group, I was blessed to have a sponsor (like a mentor) in my 50s who never judged me! She was one I could call on and get personal with when I was dealing with problems that came up that made me feel hurt, scared and angry, etc. What I found so helpful was that she put on her ears and listened. I found that to be the biggest help before ever hearing her say anything. Then she would share a similar experience and how she dealt with it and shared from the steps that are biblical. She never told me what to do but instead made suggestions on things that might help and what she did in a similar experience.

Then after talking with her, it would be good to ask the Lord what His answer was. I'm not sure I always did that, but I have learned that the Lord is faithful and nudges me in certain ways how to go about things that come up. Prayer is very important alongside listening to what others say. She is a Catholic, and I have been a blessing to her, and I pray for her needs too when they come up.

Through the years, as I have become less needy, we talk less, but we are still friends, and occasionally we chat to keep up with one another. Having her in my life has helped me from making some very big mistakes in my relationships and with my children and allowing them to grow up to take responsibility for themselves. The Lord used her in my life as a loving blessing with skin on! She was so patient and kind, and I thank God for her.

I now am sponsoring a gal in my town who is coming to the Lord gradually! She goes to church. I pray for her and ask the Lord to work Himself into her life. I am so thrilled that she wants to have and read a children's Bible at first and then later, as she gains more confidence, read the Bible. In time, maybe as she learns to trust me more, we can talk more about biblical things as I would love that, being a Coffee Break Bible Study leader.

Lorenna E (Age 30)

Having a mentor means that I get a window to see joys and challenges I may face as I get older. I've learned so much of who I want to be and who God is making me by watching mentors go before me. Sometimes their struggles and big steps of faith don't seem connected to my own life at all, but they offer me a window into God that I wouldn't be able to access on my own. Often I end up facing the very same experiences at a future date.

God sows seeds through my mentors, especially the ones I really open up to and who really open up to me, so that at a later date, those seeds help me walk through new circumstances with wisdom and grace. My faith grows when I see that God began preparing me years before for this very season, and He often chooses to do that through mentors. A loving, faith-filled mentor is crucial to growing in faith, love, peace and wisdom!

Deb A. (Author of "There's No Place Like Home: A Journey of Faith, Hope and Love" Age 63)

When I was around 7-8 years young, I had an amazing woman, Mrs. Firchow, take me under her wings.

She would take me to the small Baptist church by her home for summer VBS. God gave her to me to be the godly woman who spoke affirmations into my life. When my mom would say horrible and ugly things to me that made me feel unwanted, Mrs. F. would say beautiful affirmations of loving, kind, encouraging words to me.

I believe in the many years I struggled with identity issues, I still remembered her kind and concerned words for someone else's child. I would encourage all mothers and grandmothers who see a child who doesn't have a person in their life that speaks affirmations of love and kindness to them to take them under your wings. Help them to know and understand that it wasn't God's plan that the words of others would hurt them. Protect them with your love and words from our Father who tells them they are beautiful. One day, they may turn to God for help to be rescued from this world. I did!

Emma S. (age 38)

I have had many women in my life who have helped shape me into who I am today. There are a few that stand out as mentors.

The first would be my Grandma Alice. When I was young, she taught me to bake, sew, clean, and work hard. Grandpa and Grandma would bring us to church every Sunday because that's what they did. They loved God, served Him, and that's how we show Him we love Him back. She also taught me so much by the way she lived her life more than by words. She loved me always, even when family relationships were strained later in life.

The next would be my Aunt. When I was 16, she reached out to me at a time in life I thought no one cared about me. Family life was rough, and she took me under her wing to teach me the basics of God. The seed that had been planted in my young life was watered.

Another woman came along when I was 16: my then boyfriend's (now husband) mother, Barb. She had three sons and always wanted a daughter. From the moment we started dating, that family treated me like part of theirs and even took my three younger siblings in from time to time. I am blessed to have a great relationship with my mother-in-law still today. She has given me so much of her wisdom about raising kids, being a good wife and mother-in-law.

There are so many other women who have impacted me over the years. I am so thankful and pray that I would one day also be a woman who impacts others for Christ Jesus.

My Mentor by Anita van der Elst (age 63)

I've always loved to read. The ability to read came early for me, even before I started going to school. One of my fave books as a child was a Bible story book. Hardbound in a navy blue, fabric-like cover, and about three inches thick, it provided coverage of Old Testament and New Testament Scripture in narrative form with a few color illustrations thrown in here and there. I read it several times.

Sitting quietly in church for hours at a time posed no problem for me as long as I had something to read. The only thing available was my little KJV Bible so as young as age eight or nine, I was plowing through it, including all those major and minor prophets, and getting my mind boggled. The end result was familiarity with the stories, but not a whole lot of understanding.

Accepting Jesus as my Savior at age ten set me on a journey that continues to this day. But reading the Bible became a practice that mostly felt like a chore. I knew in my head that it was God's Word but didn't feel like it spoke to me personally, or that I could relate to it, or that it could affect my life in everyday practical ways.

Then along came Lois, a woman about twenty years older than I am. We met in a small church in Southern California when I was in my early forties. In getting to know her, we would talk about books we'd read and enjoyed. Then I found out that she had taken a course in Bible studies—the Bethel series, I think it was called. I asked her if it would be possible to get together on a one-on-one basis to talk about how to make the Bible personally applicable. She was delighted. Her advice to me was first to acknowledge the Holy Spirit's presence and invite His guidance, then to read with an open heart but a questioning mind. What was the setting of the part of the Bible I was reading? Who was speaking? Who was it written to or for? Why was this information included? What might it be like if I had been there at the time? How might I take what was there and apply it to my life? And if there was something that didn't make sense to me, make a note of it. She suggested I read from a variety of Bible versions and keep a journal of questions, "aha" moments and insights. We met a couple times a month to share a cup of tea and to go over anything I wanted to share from my journal and she would share of her vast store of Biblical knowledge. This process brought life to my Bible reading and to my soul.

Lois also encouraged me to put myself into the scene of whatever unfolded on the page. Be one of the people in the crowd, or at the table, or in the battle. Maybe even write a story about it. A published author herself, she became my mentor in the area of writing as well. She led a writers' critiquing group that I was in for awhile, and we also met often one-on-one to talk about writing. It was through her that I had an opportunity to submit a devotional for a book compilation—and it was accepted.

We worked together on several writing projects and other areas of ministry at church over the years. Being mentored while serving on a team added another level and it came with a lasting friendship. Even though we live in different states now, we stay in touch, and I will always be grateful for her support and encouragement.

Gio (age 16)

There are many times in my life that I have felt like no one in this world understood me. I felt as if I was all alone in this cruel world and there wasn't anyone that I could fully trust. I came upon Launch Pad my 8th grade year and I started going out to a youth group at Sterry Memorial Church in Roswell. It was in January of 2015 when my life changed. I accepted Jesus Christ in my life and I have been very grateful since that day. I met some incredibly amazing people that are just as crazy for Jesus as I am. To this present day, I still face struggles because that's part of the everyday life, although I wouldn't be able to get through these obstacles without some of the most precious and great women that I have met along my path.

Growing up as a teen is challenging because you're figuring out who you are and what you want to be in life. For me, my life would not be the same without the advice and talks that I have with my mentors. Holly Kaiser is a huge role model to me. She is the youth group leader at Sterry. Because of her, I look at everything from a different perspective. My faith has grown more than I ever thought it could. I know that I and many others go out to her for help in times of need and she will always be there at any time. No matter what she has going on with her life, if you call her and need to talk, she will go out of her comfort zone for anyone. It is truly a blessing to have someone like Holly.

Seeing how passionate and loving Holly is towards the Lord gives me joy of knowing that there is a God who loves and forgives us for our mistakes. She taught me that it's okay to make mistakes, but never forget that the Lord will always be there for you. Of course, there are other wonderful women who help me out, but Holly is a special one. She was once a teen too and knows all about that stuff. The fact that I can count on her and know she will not judge me is awesome.

This world is full of temptation and it is really easy to fall into it. I know it is my own duty to grow in my faith, but I definitely would love to give a shout out to Holly for always giving me motivation to do my best and serve our Heavenly Father. I admire and aspire to be like her when I am older. I don't think I have ever and will ever encounter a time where I will be lost in my faith. Because I know my faith keeps growing every day and I know people like Holly are put in my life for a reason, to let me know that I am not alone.

BIBLIOGRAPHY

"Agape" http://www.gotquestions.org/agape-love.html

"Confidence" http://www.biblestudytools.com/dictionary/confidence/

Contrast chart from page 63. *http://www.biblestudymanuals.net/love.htm*

"Covenant Marriage." http://covenantmarriage.com/what-is-a-marriage-covenant/ Copyright © 2017 Covenant Marriage Movement. April 17,2017

"Covenant." http://www.biblestudytools.com/dictionary/covenant. Dictionaries - Baker's Evangelical Dictionary of Biblical Theology - Covenant M.G. Easton M.A., D.D., Illustrated Bible Dictionary, Third Edition, published by Thomas Nelson, 1897 April 17,2017

"Definition of covenant" https://www.merriam-webster.com/dictionary/covenant© 2017 Merriam-Webster, Incorporated April 17,2017

Orr, James, M.A., D.D. General Editor. "Entry for 'CONFIDENCE'". "International Standard Bible Encyclopedia". 1915 April 17,2017

"Eros" ThoughtCo https://www.thoughtco.com/eros-romantic-love-in-the-bible-363367 April 17,2017

"[**hahy**-m*uh* n] **hymen."** http://www.dictionary.com/browse/hymen

"helper (Hb. 'ezer)"
http://www.preceptaustin.org/hebrew_word_study_on_help#eze Help - Hebrew Word Study. 08/20/2016 April 17,2017

"Insecure" http://www.dictionary.com/browse/insecure © 2017 Dictionary.com, LLC. April 17, 2017

"Phileō"
https://www.blueletterbible.org/lang/lexicon/lexicon.cfm?t=KJV&strongs=G5368
April 17, 2017

"Perversion per·ver·sion."
https://www.bing.com/search?q=perverfsion&qs=n&form=QBRE&sp=-1&pq=perverfsion&sc=8-11&sk=&cvid=B3D845F414224B0A864780557A7AD107

April 17, 2017

"Reverence" http://www.biblestudytools.com/dictionary/reverence/ April 17.2017

"Should all mothers be stay-at-home moms?"
https://www.gotquestions.org/stay-at-home-mom.html © Copyright 2002-2017 Got Questions Ministries April 17, 2017

"SOUND'NESS, n." http://av1611.com/kjbp/kjv-dictionary/sound.html The King James Bible Page Webster's American Dictionary of the English Language, 1828. April 17, 2017

"Storge" ThoughtCo https://www.thoughtco.com/what-is-storge-love-700698
April 17, 2017

"Submit"=Submit https://www.connectingsingles.com/forum 3 213295 1/original greek biblical definition of submit.htm Theresa4tgl

ABOUT THE AUTHOR

Elaine Oostra is the author of One Brick at a Time: Breaking Down Walls of Bitterness. She has studied the Bible for 20 years through Precept Ministries, an in-depth Bible class. It prepared her for what God had in store for her. Elaine is a speaker for women's groups. She serves in different youth ministries, including Launch Pad Ministries, a Christian release time class for middle and high school students. She has also served as a youth leader for nine years in her church. For the past 13 years, she has had, and continues to have, Bible studies in her home for high school girls. God has given her a passion and gift for teaching the youth.

Elaine has a passion for boldly teaching the uncompromising truths of the gospel. She desires for others to know God intimately and hunger for His Word, to then take the Word and share it with others. She desires for all believers to have discernment when a false gospel is being preached and to stand firm in God's Word.

Elaine and her husband have been married for 44 years (2017) and are self-employed farmers. They have four children, and four in-laws (love) children, 16 grandchildren, 5 step-grandchildren, and one great-grandchild who are the delights of their hearts!

The joy of her heart is to see ALL come to a saving knowledge of Jesus Christ.

www.ingramcontent.com/pod-product-compliance
Lightning Source LLC
Chambersburg PA
CBHW081630040426
42449CB00014B/3250

* 9 7 8 0 9 9 7 2 3 1 6 2 5 *